A Pocket Guide to Correct
Punctuation

Second Edition

by
Robert Brittain

BARRON'S EDUCATIONAL SERIES, INC.
New York • London • Toronto • Sydney

Second Edition published in 1990 by Barron's Educational Series, Inc.
First Edition published in 1982 by Barron's Educational Series, Inc.
Title in U.S.A., *A Pocket Guide to Correct Punctuation*.

© Copyright Robert Brittain 1981
Title in England: "The Good Punctuation Guide"
Published by Charles Skilton, Ltd.

© Copyright 1990 by Barron's
Educational Series, Inc., pages 108–119.

All inquiries should be addressed to:
Barron's Educational Series, Inc.
250 Wireless Boulevard
Hauppauge, New York 11788

Library of Congress Catalog Card. No. 90-685
International Standard Book No. 0-8120-4404-5

Library of Congress Cataloging in Publication Data

Brittain, Robert Edward, 1908–
    A pocket guide to correct punctuation/by Robert Brittain. —
2nd ed.
        p.   cm.
    Rev. ed. of: Good punctuation guide. 1982.
    ISBN 0-8120-4404-5
    1. English language — Punctuation.   I. Brittain, Robert Edward,
1908-   Good punctuation guide.   II. Title.
PE1450.B714   1990
421—dc20   90-685
                                                                         CIP

PRINTED IN UNITED STATES OF AMERICA

012   5500   9 8 7 6 5 4 3 2

Contents

1 The Meaning of Punctuation   **1**
Introduction   1

2 Beginning and End Punctuation   **6**
The Capital Letter   6
The Period   8
The Question Mark   10
The Exclamation Point   11

3 A Note on Sentence Fragments   **12**

4 The Five Principal Interior Marks   **16**
The Single Comma   16
The Pair of Commas   22
The Comma-Plus-Coordinating-Conjunction   41
The Semicolon   47
The Colon   54

5 Rarely Needed Interior Marks   **59**
The Single Dash   59
The Parentheses   63
The Pair of Dashes   69

6 Punctuation of Quoted Matter   **74**
The Quotation Marks   74
The Brackets   79
The Three Dots   81
The Bar   83

7 Some Non-Punctuational Symbols   **85**
The Abbreviation Point, the Hyphen, etc.   85

8 Suggested Solutions to Exercises   **89**

9 Summary for Quick Reference   **100**

10 Exercises for Practice   **108**

1

The Meaning of Punctuation

*No man can write really well who does not
punctuate well, who cannot vitally mean
every punctuation mark as clearly and as
vigorously as he means any word.*
— *Arlo Bates: Talks on Writing English*

INTRODUCTION

The purpose of this small book is to enable you,
with the minimum of effort, to punctuate your writing
in such a way that your reader cannot fail to understand clearly and exactly what you mean. That is its sole
purpose. It is not a book designed to explain or justify
all the marks you will find in any current newspaper,
magazine, or book, to say nothing of those in all the
printed matter that has been produced in English since
the invention of printing. Its aim is simply to show you
how to use the standard marks of punctuation so as to
reveal unmistakably the meaning of your words.

If your purpose is to learn how to punctuate
your own writing effectively, it is necessary at the outset
to concentrate on your own problems and not to confuse yourself by raising irrelevant questions. You will
never learn effective punctuation by selecting sentences

at random from printed matter and asking, "What rule prompted the author or the printer to use these particular marks?"

There are several reasons why such a procedure will teach you nothing. In the first place, punctuation is not a divinely ordained thing, created before the world and enduring unchanged to all time. It is a social invention of man, and like most inventions it has undergone a number of changes and improvements since its first appearance, and will undergo more. An attempt to base your punctuation on that found in a sixteenth-century book would be as foolish as attempting to use the Wright brothers' airplane for modern transport. You may possibly learn many useful things from Shakespeare, but you cannot learn sensible punctuation from a study of early editions of his plays.

In addition to this, many of the marks used in earlier printing, and to some extent in the printing of poetry today, are not marks of *punctuation* at all. They are a kind of musical notation, designed to suggest the manner in which the material should be read aloud, just as a composer uses a group of conventional symbols to indicate the manner in which his music should be performed. To take them as marks of punctuation in the modern sense is only to create confusion. For example, the authors of a recent book on punctuation devote a number of pages to an attempt to devise rules that will justify the use of every colon in the Authorized Version of the Bible. If they would go to church instead of to the works of unimaginative grammarians, they would quickly discover that most of the colons in the Authorized Version have nothing whatever to do with punctuation: usually they are merely signals to indicate the points at which, in the antiphonal reading of the Scriptures, the minister should cease and the people should answer.

Finally, beware of rules. Grammarians have

made the rules with which they have burdened us, not by divine inspiration as to what ought to be, but by careful observation of what is. Normally, this is a most intelligent method of working. But all too often the grammarians have been content with recording and attempting to classify and explain all the bewildering uses and misuses of punctuation marks (and of symbols that *look* like punctuation marks) perpetrated by generations of harassed printers. As a result, they have confused punctuation with the "musical notation" already mentioned; they have taken seriously usages that are purely accidental or meaningless; and they have couched their laws in that complicated terminology which most people do not understand and therefore tend to forget as soon as they have memorized it. As a result, more people have been defeated by the "rules of punctuation" than have ever been helped by them.

Therefore, this book will not give you any rules at all for the use of a particular mark. Instead, it will explain what each mark of punctuation *means,* just as a dictionary explains the meaning of each word. A dictionary does not burden you with a rule or a set of rules governing the use of the word "cat," for example. It tells you simply what kind of object that three-letter word signifies, and leaves it to your own common sense to decide whether, in a given situation, you mean to refer to that animal or not.

Words are only symbols, after all, and the meaning of a given word-symbol is not established by a rule. People have simply agreed by common consent that a particular group of written letters or oral sounds shall represent or stand for a particular object or idea. There is, therefore, only one rule which you must observe if you wish your use of language to be intelligible to others: you must use a given word-symbol to represent what, by common consent, it represents to them. If you mean the animal mentioned above, you must use the word-symbol "cat"; you cannot arbitrarily write "dog," because the symbol "dog" represents, for all users of English, a quite different animal.

The same thing is true of punctuation. *A mark of punctuation is a conventional symbol used to convey to the reader a meaning not explicitly communicated by the word-symbols in the sentence.* There are several different marks, or symbols, each one representing a definite and exact meaning. Furthermore, *each mark has one meaning and only one.* And the only rule that can be laid down to govern their use is simply this: write what you mean, using each mark in its accepted significance.

The job of learning to punctuate effectively is, therefore, a relatively simple and easy one. It involves nothing more complicated than learning what the various marks mean and then getting into the habit of using them in their proper meanings. This is not to be compared with the difficulty of learning to use the word-symbols, for there are hundreds of thousands of English words, whereas we have fewer than a score of punctuation marks, of which only about ten are frequently needed in ordinary writing.

Let us not imagine, however, that because this job is easy it is not very important. If your object is to learn to communicate to your readers the exact thought that is in your mind, a mastery of punctuation is infinitely more important than a wide vocabulary. You can get along with a bare eight hundred words, which is the merest fraction of our language: it has been found possible to translate the complete Bible into such a limited vocabulary. But you cannot get along at all without punctuation. If you have ever tried to read a page of printed English from which all punctuation marks have been omitted, you will understand how basically important those little marks are. And careless use of the marks is worse than none.

Your job is further simplified by the fact that

you already know what some of the marks mean and have already formed the habit of using them properly. Although you have probably never been told what a single comma means, or how its meaning differs from that of the pair of commas, you know already what the capital letter and the period mean. Let us therefore begin with the easy and familiar marks that indicate the outside limits of the individual sentence.

2
Beginning and End Punctuation

THE CAPITAL LETTER (A, B, C, ETC.)

When you see a capital letter standing at the beginning of a group of words, you know what meaning the writer is trying to communicate to you by the use of that symbol. He is saying in effect, *"This capital letter marks the beginning of a new sentence."* Seeing it, you will understand that the first noun or pronoun you encounter after that capital letter will be, if his sentence is written in the normal order, the subject of the complete thought he is preparing to express. The meaning of this symbol is so familiar that little more need be said about it.

There is one occasion when you will see a capital letter used as a mark of punctuation within a sentence. This occurs when the sentence contains a quoted or interpolated sentence:

> **Katherine said, "Please give me a drink of water."**

Here again, however, the capital letter means that a complete sentence is beginning. It merely happens that this sentence is enclosed as a quotation within the larger one.

An Important Convention

For centuries, it was conventional in the printing of English poetry to print a capital letter at the beginning of each individual verse. The convention still persists, although many modern poets dislike it and try to get the printers to discard it.

In the following stanza, only the first capital letter is a mark of punctuation indicating the beginning of a sentence.

> *He prayeth best who loveth best*
> *All things both great and small;*
> *For the dear God who loveth us,*
> *He made and loveth all.*

The other three at the beginnings of single verses are examples of the musical notation mentioned earlier. They are intended to aid the person who speaks the poem aloud by indicating the beginning of each new rhythmic unit. Since they do not in any way affect the meaning of the sentence, they are not marks of punctuation.

Capitalization as a Mark of Spelling

In the same way, you are familiar with another conventional use of the capital letter which is not a mark of punctuation. This is the convention which prompts us to *use an initial capital letter in spelling proper names and all the principal words in formal titles,* whether of people, places, works of art, organizations, governmental divisions, calendar divisions, or indeed of anything that has a proper name. It is also customary, as you know, to capitalize words used in the salutation or close of a letter.

These conventional formalities in spelling are

universal, but one should be aware that they have no grammatical or syntactical meaning and are therefore not marks of punctuation. The only use of the capital letter for *punctuation* (that is, to communicate a meaning not clearly communicated by the word-symbols alone) is that which indicates the beginning of a sentence.

THE PERIOD (.)

What do you mean when you put a single small dot at the end of a group of words you have written? You know the answer: *a period means that this is the end of a complete statement.* It carries with it a warning to the reader that the statement is finished and must not be run together with what is to follow. The idea stated in the group of words beginning with a capital letter and ending with a period is cast in the form of a simple assertion. You do not intend to ask the reader a question, nor do you want him to feel that you are expressing the thought with great emphasis. You have simply stated it. The period tells him all this. And that is all there is to be known about the single small dot which is used as a mark of punctuation and is called a period.

Do Not Confuse the Period with the Abbreviation Point

The abbreviation point looks exactly like the punctuational period, but its function is really quite different. Actually, the abbreviation point is not a mark of punctuation at all, but a little device of spelling which we sometimes use to save time in writing certain words. It does not appear at the end of a group of words but at the end of a group of letters which are not a completed word-symbol. It is quicker to write "Mr." than to write "Mister," or "Ala." than "Alabama." These "shorthand" symbols are called abbreviations, and they are legitimate substitutes for their corresponding word-symbols. The dot which is always placed at the end of them is just a device for warning the reader that the letters composing the abbreviation are not some strange new word-symbol, but merely a short substitute for one with which he is familiar.

When initial capital letters are used as the abbreviation for a name, the abbreviation point is normally placed after each initial, as in "Y.M.C.A." During recent years, however, when so many new organizations have come into being, it has become customary in some instances to omit the abbreviation points and to write the particular capital letters together as a single word-symbol. For example, we frequently find the abbreviation for "United Nations" written simply as "UN," with no abbreviation points at all. This symbol is pronounced "you-enn," but there are many examples in which the abbreviation has actually become a new word-symbol, pronounced as such, although written with the capital initials. Thus "WAC" (Women's Army Corps, formerly "WAAC," or Women's Auxiliary Army Corps) and "WAVES" (Women's Auxiliary Volunteer Emergency Services) are pronounced as single-syllable words.

Modern usage has gone even farther in this business of creating new word-symbols from abbreviations composed of initial letters, using a capital letter for only the first initial. For example, the word-symbol "UNESCO" for "United Nations Educational, Scientific, and Cultural Organization" is sometimes spelled "Unesco." In general, the whole question of the proper spelling of such abbreviations is at present in a state of flux, and the only sound advice anyone can give you is to consult the organization concerned and be guided by its own spelling of the abbreviated name.

Note that when an abbreviation occurs at the end of a statement, the abbreviation point and the period are combined into one dot.

He lived for ten years in Boston, Mass.

But no other mark of punctuation ever absorbs the abbreviation point.

Are you referring to Salem, Ore., or to Salem, Mass.?

Another Spelling Device

There is another dot which is used as a device of spelling and which must not be confused with the period. If you wish to express in Arabic numerals such a number as "five and twenty-seven hundredths," you spell it "5.27." The decimal part of any mixed number, when it is expressed in Arabic numerals, is always spelled with this dot or "decimal point" immediately preceding the decimal fraction.

25.2 means twenty-five and two-tenths.
.005 means five-thousandths.

THE QUESTION MARK (?)

This mark, again, is so well known as to need little comment. Like the period, it means that a thought has been completely expressed, but it warns the reader that you have not expressed the thought as an assertion; instead of telling him something, you have asked him something. "He died." "He died?" The first sentence means one thing; the second means something quite different. Since the initial capital letters and the two word-symbols are exactly the same in both sentences, the difference in meaning is communicated solely by the different punctuation marks at the ends of the two sentences and this difference can be communicated in no other way known to writing and printing. If we deliver the two sentences orally, we use another kind of symbol to convey the difference in meaning: in speaking, we use the oral symbol of rising vocal inflection for the question.

THE EXCLAMATION POINT (!)

This mark means vehemence, violence, passion! If you wish one of your assertions to strike the reader's mind with a forcefulness like that with which a shout or some other emphatic tone of voice would strike his ears, place an exclamation point at the end of that assertion. This will show him that if you were talking you would *exclaim* that particular sentence with considerable emphasis.

Be very careful and rather sparing in the use of this mark, however; it can easily be overdone. A page liberally sprinkled with exclamation points produces exactly the same effect as a speech filled with shouts, grimaces, and emphatic gestures. It is perfectly legitimate and effective to lift your voice once in a while, but constant overstressing of words and sentences quickly produces an effect of hysteria. No one enjoys listening to the person who cannot describe a simple visit to the cinema without gushing and shrieking, "Oh! my dear! it was simply divine!" In the same way, it is not interesting to read prose that is filled with exclamation points.

3
A Note on Sentence Fragments

So far we have dealt only with the familiar punctuation marks that are used to indicate the beginning and ending of complete sentences. Before we proceed to examine marks used within the sentence, it would be well to take note of the fragmentary statement. Normally, for the complete expression of an idea we need a group of words that forms what is called a sentence or an independent clause. This is simply a group of words that contains a subject and a predicate and that makes sense when standing alone. There are, however, three other grammatical forms in which ideas can be stated or suggested with varying lesser degrees of completeness: the dependent clause, the phrase, and the single word. Under normal circumstances (that is, about ninety-nine times out of a hundred), ideas expressed in any of these forms do not make sense when standing alone; they must be joined , as modifiers, to the subject or the predicate of an independent clause before their meaning becomes clear. Occasionally, however, a single word or phrase, and *very rarely* even a dependent clause, communicates an idea with as much clearness as a complete sentence. The single word "Nuts!" or the comical phrase "Oh, yeah?" can on occasion be more eloquent than a dozen sentences.

How do you punctuate one of these fragmentary constructions? If it really does the job as well as a complete sentence would, treat the fragment like a sentence and place a capital letter at the beginning of it and either a period, a question mark, or an exclamation point at the end of it. If the fragment does not do the job of a complete sentence (and in the vast majority of examples it will not), either attach it as a modifer to the word in a near-by sentence which it modifies, or recast it into the form of an independent sentence and let it stand alone. For example:

> "Did you have any trouble finding the place?" "Practically none. The streets are well marked."

> Will this new plan give us more time to study? Obviously not. More recreation? That is highly debatable. More opportunity to make friends with our fellow students? No. All it offers is more waiting around between classes.

> Oh, for something difficult to get my teeth into! Easy jobs are wearing me out.

The fragments in the above examples are all as perfectly comprehensible as if they were expressed in complete sentences. They should therefore be punctuated as sentences. Below are some which cannot stand alone.

> He soon found that Nora was under the thumb of her sister. But completely.

> This is slovenly and vulgar writing, and no amount of punctuation will make these words

anything else. The only thing to do with a fragment like this is to throw it away. If you still want to increase the emphasis in the sentence, you can write, "He soon found that Nora was completely under the thumb of her sister."

Henry then proposed that we go ahead with plans for the class party with the understanding that it could be cancelled by the committee if the Principal should remain adamant. A solution that seemed to everybody present to offer the best way out of our difficulties.

Here the fragment is too long to be attached to an already cumbersome sentence. "This solution seemed . . ." will make it a sentence in its own right.

EXERCISE

In the following examples, examine each word or group of words that is punctuated like a sentence (with initial capital and terminal mark). Ask yourself simply, "Does this make sense by itself?" If it does not, how would you express the idea the writer is trying to suggest? Would you make a sentence out of it? Would you express it in two or more sentences? Would you somehow work it into a nearby sentence?

Do not worry at this point about punctuating the resulting sentences. The only purpose of this exercise is to get you to recognize a fragment when you write one, and to urge you to decide consciously whether it expresses your meaning clearly or not.

1. Children have unbelievable energy. Enough to wear out a trained athlete. And day after day, at that.
2. Mothers work a twenty-four-hour day. Meals, dishes, getting the children off to school, and without overtime pay.
3. When the bell rang, both boxers got to their feet. One briskly, the other wearily.

4. "Easy now, easy does it. Now!" cried the skipper.

5. "Where am I going? None of your business. That is, I'm going out. To Mamie's, if you must know."

6. "Who goes there? Friend or foe?"

7. What can we expect? Peace or war? Inflation or depression? These problems face the graduate today, and he cannot hope to hide from them.

8. He displayed great assurance in declaiming on modern affairs. But little knowledge.

9. I became more and more discouraged as I fell farther and farther behind. Finally having to quit school.

10. He says they're going to increase our salaries. Which is all right with me. Only how about those vacations?

11. Having been in school at the time when all my friends who were about the same age were already working at jobs, keeping regular hours, and bringing home every week some money that they had earned.

12. Everyone was ready and eager to be off. But not Alex. He had to look for his ski wax. The dope.

4

The Five Principal Interior Marks

The marks that are used for punctuation within the sentence are the ones that most people find difficult and confusing. There are several of them, and we shall discuss each in due course, but five are of major importance: the single comma, the pair of commas, the comma plus coordinating conjunction, the semicolon, and the colon.

Before you examine the first of these, you should notice very carefully that three of them involve the use of the same symbol, either alone or in combination with other symbols: the single comma, the pair of commas, and the comma plus coordinating conjunction. Grammarians group all these together as "commas" and give some fifteen to twenty rules for their use. They are, however, three completely separate and distinct marks, or punctuational devices. Each has one meaning and only one, so that instead of fifteen things to learn you have only three.

THE SINGLE COMMA (,)

The single comma occurs with comparative rarity; in fact, there are only two situations where it is generally used, and in both of them it has the same meaning. One of these situations is found in the following sentence:

To err is human; to forgive, divine.

Upon examination, you will see that in this sentence the comma is inserted in place of the word "is," which is omitted. The single comma means, therefore, at this point there is omitted from the sentence a small element which the reader can easily supply for himself.

Mary wore a red dress; Helen, a blue one.

He began to sing, not exactly a song but a kind of tuneless drone.

(An element like "something which was" is omitted.)

Many nations have striven by different means to achieve democracy: France, by a bloody political revolution; the United States, by a war of liberation followed by the establishment of a constitutional republic; England, by a long series of gradual reforms and reorganizations.

The second situation in which the single comma is used occurs when a coordinating conjunction is omitted from a series of words or phrases in the same construction.

A tall, thin, angular man walked slowly into the room.

We demand an end to tyranny, a breaking of bonds we have endured too long.

In sentences like the last example, a careful writer would on occasion use a colon instead of a single comma; sometimes he would even use a single dash. Either one would be a perfectly clear and explicit mark [see the discussion of the colon and of the single dash on pp. 54 and 59], but you should note carefully that the *meaning* of the sentence would be different in each case. You must not think that one mark is "right" and another "wrong"; your choice should depend entirely on what you mean. The example given, when punctuated with the single comma, means simply that the "and" which you would expect between the two phrases has, for purposes of rhetorical effect, been omitted.

Usually if only two elements are joined, the conjunction is written and there is consequently no comma, but when several elements are joined in a series the repetition of the conjunction produces an unpleasant, rambling effect. In this situation, the conjunction is omitted and the reader is warned of the omission by the single comma.

The house was large and handsome.

The house was large, handsome, imposing.

The house was large, handsome, and imposing.

The last example given raises an interesting question of usage. Some editors punctuate it as it appears above. Others print it this way:

The house was large, handsome and imposing.

Logically, those who use the second method are right. They could argue that since the single comma means a small element is here omitted, it should not be used when the element is not omitted.

There is, however, an argument on the other side. Those who use both the comma and the conjunction between the last two elements in a series might point out that if you write, "The house was large, handsome and imposing," it looks to your reader as if you were telling him *two* things about the house (*one,* "large"; *two,* "handsome and imposing"), whereas in reality you are trying to tell *three* separate and distinct things about it.

In the sentence given, it does not make much difference; your reader will understand what you mean regardless of which you use, and you will find excellent editorial authority for either punctuation. However, there are instances where the single commas will make a difference in your meaning. If one of the elements in your series is a compound, for example, you will certainly need to separate the elements very carefully with commas.

He had red, blue and yellow, green, and gold balloons.

If the sentence is punctuated thus, the reader knows that there were four kinds of ballons, whereas if you write "red, blue and yellow, green and gold balloons," he does not know whether there were four color schemes or three (or possibly five!).

Therefore, it seems to be better to insert the extra single comma between the last two elements in a series, even though the conjunction is also inserted for rhetorical smoothness. It is not strictly logical, but it cannot be too often repeated that punctuation is not a matter of logical "rules" but simply a system of conventional symbols used to make the meaning of written language clear to the reader. If you always put in the extra single comma, you will never confuse anybody; if you leave it out, there are many situations in which you will confuse everybody.

A Spelling Device

There is one kind of word-symbol in which a mark that looks exactly like a punctuational single comma is used as a device of spelling. It occurs when you write any number larger than 999 in Arabic numerals.

1,365   **27,090**   **4,728,256**

Notice that this little symbol is not a mark of punctuation. It does not occur between word-symbols but within one symbol. Like the dot which indicates the decimal fraction of a mixed number, it is purely a trick of spelling.

EXERCISE

The following exercise, like all that you will find in later pages of this book, should be taken simply as a set of suggested materials on which you may practice to develop habits of expressing clearly and exactly what *you* mean. Many of the examples will contain ideas in which you may have no interest and which you would never care to express at all. Others will be expressed in words and phrases that are not natural to you. Such shortcomings are inevitable in any prepared set of exercises. But you can learn a good bit by working on them, just the same, provided that you work with some imagination and common sense. The best general plan of work I can suggest is this:

a. Read the example given, and try to determine as clearly as you can what the writer of it was trying to communicate.

b. See if you can, by inserting marks of punctuation, make that meaning clear.

c. If you cannot, rewrite the sentence in your own way, punctuating it to make *your* meaning clear. Do not hesitate to do such rewriting; the objective is not to use the "correct" punctuation, but to express what you mean.

d. When you have produced what you think is a clear sentence, *be able to explain every mark of punctuation you have used, and to show how that mark reveals the meaning you wish to convey.* For example, "Since this fragment makes sense when standing alone, I have punctuated it like a sentence." Or, "I have put an exclamation point at the end of this group of words because the sentence ends here and I want it spoken with emphasis." Or, "This single comma means that the word 'and' is omitted."

1. We have fought with courage; our opponents with guile.

2. It was a cold clear day.

3. There was really nothing to do on the island except to swim to hunt or to fish.

4. He was very old withered and brittle as an autumn leaf and as ready to be blown away.

5. It embraces such factors as food supplies animal enemies and even social traditions customs and laws.

6. The bodies of many animals are better adapted than man's for self-defense escape or hunting. Yet man has learned how to beat the polar bear the hare the hawk and the tiger at their particular tricks.

7. The King of Norway the Queen of England and Head of the Commonwealth and the President of France were at the conference.

8. Wynken Blynken and Nod were sued for copyright infringement together separately and severally.

9. His sisters and his cousins and his aunts also went below.

10. The deaf the dumb and the blind came thronging to meet the new swami.

11. How many pesos equal one dollar? How many francs one peso? How many lire one franc?

12. Two weeks have been spent in planning; four in getting the material together; sixteen in consulting with various and sundry; and yet the work is not started.

13. I've been so busy lately arranging for the hall the printing of the tickets the hiring of the musicians the publicity in the newspapers and magazines and on the billboards that I've not been able to answer your kind thoughtful letter.

THE PAIR OF COMMAS (, . . . ,)

The pair of commas is used more frequently than any other mark of interior punctuation. For this reason, it is perhaps the most important single punctuational symbol we possess. Like all the others, it has one meaning and only one, but because of the structure of our language this single meaning occurs in a wide variety of syntactical situations. You will probably need to spend more time and thought in mastering the pair of commas than in learning to handle all the other marks combined, but you will also be more richly rewarded.

The first thing to fix in your mind concerning the pair of commas is that it is *one* punctuational mark. It is composed of two symbols, of course, and these two are always separated from each other by a word or a group of words. Yet these two symbols are *not* two single commas: they *never* indicate that at two points a word or phrase has been omitted from the sentence. They have no meaning at all until they are recognized for what they are, that is, two symbols which form together *one single mark* of punctuation, just as the two letter-symbols "b" and "e" mean nothing until they are joined together to form the single word-symbol "be."

Some examples of sentences containing the pair of commas should make this clear.

> **John, who never stopped to think before he acted, ran off immediately towards the firehouse.**

> **Overseas trade, upon which the colonies depended for their livelihood, was now cut off.**

> **Mr. Robinson, whose shop was in the next building, came down the steps.**

After the words "John," "trade," and "Mr. Robinson," no single small element like "and" or "but" is omitted. If you try to put one in, you will make hash of the sentences. Similarly, you cannot insert an "and" or some similar small element before the words "ran," "was," or "came" without producing something meaningless. It is clear that you are not dealing with two single commas in each sentence but with an entirely different mark of punctuation: namely, with a pair of commas set around a word or words that make up an element of the sentence.

What does this pair of commas mean? In the first place, it is evident that you could omit the whole element enclosed by the pair of commas and still have left a clear and sensible sentence. "John ran off immediately towards the firehouse." "Overseas trade was now cut off." "Mr. Robinson came down the steps." The element enclosed within the pair of commas is *not grammatically essential* to the construction of a clear and meaningful sentence. Take it out and you still have left a subject, a verb, and a verb complement, and these three elements alone a.. sufficient to make a complete and clear statement. Therefore we can begin to define this mark of punctuation by saying that *the element enclosed within a pair of commas is not grammatically essential to the construction of a sentence.*

But this is not all. If you will look at these sentences carefully again, you will notice that each of the nonessential elements within its pair of commas separates a subject from its verb. Now if one is using the English language, a separation of the subject from its verb is a pretty serious matter. The reason for this is simple: the only clue we have to understanding the function of any word in an English sentence is the *position* in which we find that word. Any one reading a sentence in English expects the first noun or pronoun he encounters to be the subject of the action to be described, and he expects that subject to be followed immediately by a verb which will tell him what the subject is doing. If that expected order is changed or interrupted, he becomes confused. "John hit Mary" makes sense to him; "John Mary hit" does not. "Mary hit John" would also make sense, but an entirely different sense. "The young *man* on the new motorbike accidentally *hit one* of the girls who were standing on the pavement" is also clear: the subject, verb, and object are in the expected order, and all the other words are essential modifiers and are placed where they belong, each next to the word it modifies.

The normal order in the arrangement of an English sentence is of fundamental importance. The only way you can avoid confusing and misleading your readers is by observing it scrupulously. This order is unchanging; in every normal sentence it must be: *subject* with its essential modifiers, *verb* with its essential modifiers, *object* or *verb complement* with its essential modifiers. We must perforce write sentences like the following if we expect to be understood:

The old (essential modifiers of subject)	man	*in the chair by the window* (essential modifiers of subject)
suddenly (essential modifier of verb)	laid	*upon his knees* (essential modifier of verb)
the illustrated (essential modifiers of object)	magazine	*which he had been reading.* (essential modifier of object)

If we change this order, we either change the meaning of the sentence or reduce it to meaningless gibberish.

The illustrated magazine suddenly laid upon his knees the old man in the chair which he had been reading by the window.

or

In the chair which he had been reading the magazine by the window upon his knees laid the old man suddenly.

The reason the first of these examples seems so ridiculous is that any one of us, seeing "The illustrated magazine" at what appears to be the beginning of a sentence, naturally assumes that it is to be the subject of a verb, and when we see the verb "laid" immediately following it, we suppose that it represents what the magazine did. When this verb is followed by "the old man," the entire group of words can only be describing a fantastic impossibility.

We cannot escape the iron necessity to arrange our words in the normal order of the English sentence. Whether we like it or not, the meaning of word-symbols in English depends upon their position in the sentence, and if we wish our readers to know what we mean, we must place each element where they expect it to be. We must write sentences like this:

Helen began to cry when Mrs. Jones corrected her.

But must we? You have probably already begun to ask, "Is there no possible escape from this inexorable law?" The answer is that like many other laws it cannot be openly flouted, but it can be complied with in several ways. In certain communities in Connecticut, there is a law which prohibits the citizen from walking into his backyard whenever he feels like it and burning trash in the open. But if there is trash in his yard which he desires to burn, he is not obliged to let it lie there until it rots or blows away. He telephones the local fire warden and tells his story. The fire warden then checks the weather, and if there is no dangerous wind blowing he explains to the citizen certain conditions which he must observe: he must have at least two people to guard the fire, and they must be equipped with a supply of water in case the flames should start to spread. If the citizen complies with these regulations, he may burn his trash.

The same kind of compliance is possible in regard to the law which says, "You must not change in any way the normal order of the elements in an English sentence." If you think you can get a more effective sentence by changing this normal order, you may do so, *provided that you explain your intention clearly to everybody concerned and set the proper guards around your violation* to prevent it from destroying the meaning of your sentence. Thus, if the sentence "Helen began to cry when Mrs. Jones corrected her" strikes you as a dull way of expressing your meaning, you can say exactly the same thing in a slightly more interesting way by writing this:

Helen, when Mrs. Jones corrected her, began to cry.

You have not really violated the law which says that a subject must be followed immediately by its verb. It is true that you have changed this expected order by inserting another element between them. But since no reader expects to see a mark of punctuation between a subject and its verb, you have given him clear and distinct warning of your intention by setting a pair of commas around the misplaced element. At the same time, that pair of commas acts as a guard to prevent the inserted element from spreading over into the rest of the sentence and distorting the meaning.

We have already determined that *the pair of commas means that the element which it encloses is not grammatically essential to the construction of the sentence*. Now we can expand this meaning by adding that *the enclosed element changes in some way the normal order of the sentence*.

It is necessary to remember that the pair of commas means both these things. Check back on the examples already given to be sure you understand that this is true.

> **Helen, when Mrs. Jones corrected her, began to cry.**

What is essential to the construction of a sentence? A subject, a verb, and usually either an object or a complement to complete the meaning of the verb satisfactorily.

> **Helen** *(subject)* **began** *(verb)* **to cry** *(complement)*.

Those four words are all that are essential to the construction of a clear sentence. The clause "when Mrs. Jones corrected her" not only interrupts the normal order of subject-verb, but also is not an essential modifier of any of the three indispensable elements, and thus it could be omitted entirely without destroying the grammatical construction.

Again, take the sentence:

> **John, who never stopped to think before he acted, ran off immediately towards the firehouse.**

It is clear that the clause "who never stopped to think before he acted" changes the normal order of the sentence, since it separates the subject from its verb. It is equally clear that it is not essential to the construction of the sentence, for "John ran off immediately towards the firehouse" makes perfect sense by itself.

But let us suppose that you have a sentence like this:

> **One who never stops to think before he acts is apt to do some foolish things.**

Here, you will notice, there is no pair of commas around the clause "who never stops to think before he acts," yet it stands between the subject, "one," and its verb, "is." Why is it not enclosed within a pair of commas? The answer is to be found by asking two other questions. (1) Is it essential to the construction of a meaningful sentence? Yes, it is. If you omit it, you have left only "One is apt to do some foolish things," and that does not make complete sense because we do not know whom you are talking about. The dependent clause is an *essential* modifier of the subject. (2) Does the dependent clause change the normal order in this sentence? No, it does not. The normal order is: subject *with its essential modifiers,* verb with its essential modifiers, object or complement with its essential modifiers. Since the clause is an essential modifier of the subject, it is exactly where it belongs.

The same principle applies to essential or non-essential modifiers of any one of the three indispensable elements.

> **He despised everybody who had less money than he.**
> The clause "who had less money than he" is an essential modifier of the object, "everybody." The snob who is the subject of this sentence did not despise everybody in the world, but only those who were less rich than himself.

> **He looked upon Mrs. Robbins, who had less money than he, with ill-concealed contempt.**
> Here the clause "who had less money than he" is not essential to our understanding because we know that the object of his contempt is Mrs. Robbins, a definite and clearly defined person. The nonessential modifier is merely put in as a kind of parenthetical explanation.

**An evil soul producing holy witness
is like a villain with a smiling cheek.**

Not every evil soul is like a smiling villain: only the one who produces holy witness, and only while he is in the act of doing it.

If you blow upon this wheel, even though it be only a breath, you will set it turning.

Although the dependent clause does modify the verb, it is not an essential modifier; since it is also out of its normal position, it needs the pair of commas around it.

Very often you will find that a modifier, although clearly essential to the meaning of your sentence, is just as clearly out of its normal position. Does the fact that the normal order is changed make it necessary to use the pair of commas around the misplaced element? No, not unless that element is also grammatically nonessential.

At the end of the road stood Dr. Morgan's house.

Here the order is exactly the reverse of the normal one. Yet every element is essential. No pair of commas is needed, and none should be used.

EXERCISE

1. Music when soft voices die
   Vibrates in the memory.
   Odors when sweet violets sicken
   Live within the sense they quicken.
2. Peter who was seven and Nora who was two took turns on the sled.
3. Peter the Hermit was a far cry from Peter the Prior.
4. And so ends the story of Hansel and Gretel.

5. Henry with his typical disregard or unawareness of the consequences blustered on.

6. The Twentieth Air Force which dropped the atom bomb operated from the Marianas. The plane that carried the bomb was a special B-29.

7. He prayeth best who loveth best
   All things both great and small.

8. "I want the following at the pool tomorrow: Joe who admits he needs the practice; Fred who won't admit it; and all those who think they are too good for the drudgery of training."

9. Can you remember the bell that used to ring whenever there was a fire?

10. After many a summer dies the swan.

11. Enemies and detractors who do not know a hawk from a handsaw will try to break your confidence in yourself.

12. The boy upon hearing of the death of his adored elder brother broke into a long uncontrollable sob.

Enclosing Transitional Words and Phrases

It should now be clear that *the pair of commas means the element enclosed within this mark of punctuation is not essential to the grammatical structure of the sentence and is placed in such a position that it interrupts or changes the normal order.* If you have understood this meaning thoroughly, and have seen how it applies in the situations already illustrated, you should now proceed to consider other situations in which this mark is used to convey the same meaning.

You frequently have occasion to write sentences like these:

> **This book, for example, gives a good summary of the question.**

> **The girl in the blue dress, on the other hand, dances very well.**

Before we take up that problem, however, we should be wise to finish with this one.

The phrases "for example," "on the other hand," and "however" are three of a large number of words and phrases employed in English for the sole purpose of forming a bridge from one idea to another. Grammarians call them "transitional words and phrases." They never have any other function. They cannot be subjects, verbs, objects, or verb complements, nor can they modify any of these elements. Therefore it should be clear that they are never essential to the grammatical construction of a sentence. They have no *grammatical* function at all; they are merely rhetorical devices used to obtain a smooth flow of thought. Do they also change the normal order of the sentence? Yes, they do. Since they have no normal position in the sentence, they are always out of place, no matter where they appear. They always separate two elements which belong together. For these two reasons, whenever you use a transitional word or phrase, always warn your reader that you are doing so by enclosing it within a pair of commas.

EXERCISE

1. The point then is to anticipate your partner's bid.
2. The job you see is to reload immediately.
3. He made up his mind therefore to hold his tongue and come what might to think things through alone.
4. "I'll go easy if you know what I mean if you'll reconsider buying the ticket."
5. The trouble you'll agree lies in ourselves not in our stars.
6. And who come to think of it will be ready to carry on in your place?

Enclosing Elements in Apposition

Another situation involving grammatically nonessential elements which interrupt or change the normal word order is illustrated in such sentences as these:

> **He lived in Boston, Massachusetts, for three years.**

> **Her youngest daughter was born on January 27, 1938, at four o'clock in the morning.**

> **The offices of the company are located at 448 Barrow Street, New York, N.Y. 10014.**

The elements enclosed within pairs of commas are all conventionally regarded as parenthetical. Notice that in the first sentence the word "Massachusetts" stands between two essential modifiers of the verb, which should normally be together. One might consider that this word is essential to your meaning, since it is important to know which of several Bostons you are talking about. But you should notice carefully that it is not *grammatically* essential to the construction of the sentence. It has become an accepted convention of English writing to regard elements like this as completely parenthetical. The name of a geographical area immediately following the name of some locality within that area, the name of a year immediately following a date within that year, and the various elements of an address are all examples.

A more obvious situation demanding the pair of commas is found in such sentences as the following:

> **Dr. John Doe, President of Blanks College, made the principal address of the evening.**

> **The chairman requested the delegate from the Civil Liberties Union, Judge Henry Robinson, to report on the work of his organization.**

The phrases which are enclosed within pairs of commas are said by grammarians to be "in apposition" with the elements that precede them. But you need not trouble yourself to memorize another term. All that is necessary is to note that although they modify the preceding element they are not essential modifiers, because the element is completely clear and definite without them. This situation is really just a variant of the one you found in the sentence, "John, who never stopped to think before he acted, ran off immediately towards the firehouse." "John" is one definite person; so is "Dr. John Doe," or "the delegate from the Civil Liberties Union." Your reader does not require the extra explanatory phrase in order to know whom you are talking about.

EXERCISE

1. God bless you each and every one large small and intermediate.

2. His generosity or rather his recklessness is a constant source of irritation to his wife.

3. Transcendentalism the philosophy that has one foot in Platonism and the other in Christianity depends on poetry for its full definition.

4. President Roosevelt said that the date of December 7 1941 when the Japanese attacked Pearl Harbor would live in infamy.

5. The blow fell on the 30th of September in 1949.

6. R. H. Davis reporter and soldier of fortune seemed to enjoy the panoply of war.

7. Mr. Abernethy the new minister for colonies did not relinquish his old post of commissioner of the bureau of seed distribution.

8. And why should I listen to this of all the demands just and unjust made upon my time?

9. I cannot grant you a student a favor such as this one which I have refused Dr. Gammerton my own colleague.

10. The company is one of the oldest Gary, Ind. enterprises.

In connection with the use of a pair of commas around words in apposition, you should notice again that careful usage of punctuation marks can often greatly affect the meaning and effectiveness of your writing. Consider the difference between the two following sentences:

Several different marks, or symbols, are used.

Several different marks or symbols are used.

In the first of these examples, the writer intends the reader to understand that "marks" and "symbols" are simply two alternative words for the same thing. He thinks that either one would describe accurately the entire group of things he is talking about. When he offers the reader the choice in terminology, he is interrupting the normal order of his sentence by inserting a nonessential element, and the pair of commas warns the reader of this. In the second example, the meaning is quite different. To the writer of this sentence, "marks" and "symbols" have two quite different meanings, and he is trying to make the reader understand that he is describing a group of things, some of which he would call "marks" and some, "symbols." Of course, he would have done better to write "marks *and* symbols," but since he chose the other wording he must omit the pair of commas to make his meaning as clear as possible.

In the same way, you sometimes interrupt one of your own sentences by addressing directly the person or persons to whom you are talking. This, again, changes the normal order of your sentence by the insertion of an element which is not essential to that sentence.

This point, ladies and gentlemen, is very important.

Come here, John, and give me a hand with this box.

Enclosing a Direct Quotation

Always the situation that demands a pair of commas is the same: a nonessential element interrupts or changes the normal word order. There is only one exception to this and it has become so firmly fixed by convention that we normally do not think of it as an exception. It is the convention which makes us regard a direct quotation as a nonessential, interruptive element.

Johnny shouted, "Last one in is a rotten egg," and dived into the pool

Actually the entire element within the quotation marks is simply the essential object of "shouted" and is therefore exactly where it belongs in the normal word order. The quotation marks are enough to show that it is one element, and the pair of commas seems quite unnecessary. But for some unknown reason, writers and printers of English have always placed a pair of commas around such direct quotations, and it is probably too late in the day to attempt to change the custom.

Enclosing Elements at Beginning or End of Sentence

Finally, there is a very important and extremely common situation which we have not discussed. By this time, it should be firmly fixed in your mind that the pair of commas is a signal that warns the reader that the grammatically nonessential element it encloses interrupts or changes the normal word order in your sentence. "But what happens," you may ask, "if this nonessential element comes at the beginning or end of my sentence?" Let us see.

As a matter of fact, the situation is not altered by the fact that the nonessential element comes at the beginning of this sentence.

> Neither does the placing of this element at the end of the sentence alter the situation, as in this example.

> The chairman then recognized Mr. Brown, the delegate from Indiana.

Now many honest people looking at these sentences would at first protest that neither one of them contains a pair of commas, for they can see only one comma in each. That is true: only one is visible. But is it therefore a single comma? Of course not. Nothing is omitted from either sentence. The phrases "as a matter of fact," "as in this example," and "the delegate from Indiana" are grammatically nonessential. Do they interrupt or change the normal order of the English sentence? They certainly do. In the normal order, an English sentence begins with either the subject or an essential modifier of the subject; it ends with either the object or verb complement or an essential modifier of one of these. Any other element in the initial or final position is out of its normal position in the sentence.

Why do you see only one part of the pair of commas? Simply because it would look ridiculous to write:

> ,As a matter of fact,
>
> *or*
>
> ,as in this example,.
>
> *or*
>
> ,the delegate from Indiana,.

Generally, two marks of punctuation coming together appear useless and confusing. We have noticed that when a sentence ends with an abbreviation a single dot performs the function of both the abbreviation point and the period. The same principle applies here. *When two marks of punctuation come at the same point, the less emphatic one is usually absorbed into the more emphatic one.* Since marks that indicate the beginning and ending of complete sentences are more emphatic than those which clarify the meaning of small elements within the sentence, the capital letter or the period absorbs half of the pair of commas.

You will find the same principle operative in some of the following sentences:

EXERCISE

1. Your ancestry cannot help you whatever it is.
2. If you feel whatever your background that you cannot stand and say Amen then you must indeed search your heart.
3. Of a' the airts the wind can blaw I dearly like the west.
4. Of the thirteen who led the attack the first two who died were the bravest.
5. To that question there is no answer the old professor wiping his glasses replied.
6. The cook bellowed Come and get it! in his belly-deep roar.
7. All right then let it slide said the weary officer of the day.
8. Although he advanced through calculation or shrewdness his brother owed his promotion to outstanding courage or recklessness one might call it.
9. They were forced to act like beasts and not like men or women.
10. Although you prefer the thin sliced lamb I like the beef however you slice it.
11. Came the dawn and there was Miss Mary Moppet who was the child star of 1936.
12. The party of the first part hereby contracts to convey to the party of the second part and to his heirs or assigns wherever they may be all property real or personal on that site.
13. All he could say when he won the puppy was "Gosh!"
14. No you can't take it with you was the platitude he ended with.

This covers all the major situations in which you will need to enclose an element within a pair of commas in order to make clear to your reader the meaning of your sentence. Since the pair of commas is the most important and most commonly used of all the marks of interior punctuation you will find constant occasion to use it.

Omission of the Pair of Commas

Once you have firmly established the habit of placing a pair of commas around a nonessential element which interrupts or changes the normal order of the English sentence, you will be prepared to consider a few situations in modern prose writing in which this mark of punctuation may safely be omitted. You are doubtless aware that the tendency of modern writers is to make considerably less use of punctuation than their predecessors did. One reason for this, of course, is that we have ceased to use the "musical notation" that was once fashionable, probably because most modern prose is designed to be read silently, to be taken in by the eye and not by the ear. These marks were never marks of actual punctuation, in the sense that they clarified meaning, and today they have about disappeared from printing. A more important reason for the diminishing amount of punctuation in modern writing is that our writers are learning to construct their sentences in such a way that the word-symbols themselves communicate the meaning clearly. A well-written sentence normally needs very little interior punctuation.

There is a tendency in modern writing, however, to go beyond this. You will sometimes find it possible and even desirable to omit the pair of commas from around some element that is nonessential and that is so placed in the sentence as to change the normal order. But the careful writer who makes this omission *does it only when there is no possible chance of the reader's misunderstanding the meaning.*

What situations fulfill this requirement? In ordinary contemporary English prose, there are only two.

1. Transitional words and phrases are normally enclosed within a pair of commas because they are grammatically nonessential, and because, since they have no normal position in the sentence, they always change the normal order, no matter where they appear. Sometimes, however, one of these transitional elements is so small and fits so easily into the sentence that no reader is likely to be disturbed by the separation of the two elements it stands between. In such situations, the pair of commas is often omitted.

> **He was therefore elected without further debate.**

"Therefore" cannot be a verb complement following "was"; it is evident to the reader that the order must be "was elected." The function of the word "therefore" is clear without the pair of commas to call attention to it. It fits so smoothly here as to seem almost an adverb, an essential modifier. But notice that in another position it needs the pair of commas.

> **He was elected, therefore, without further debate.**

You should notice that certain words function sometimes as transitions and at other times as modifiers. With such words, it is essential to use the pair of commas when the word is purely transitional.

> **The fields, on the one hand, are green, but the trees already show the effects of drought.**

> **The fields on the one hand are green, but those on the other are beginning to turn brown.**

2. Sometimes the wording itself shows the reader clearly that the order is changed or interrupted by a nonessential element. If this happens, no pair of commas is necessary, for punctuation is needed only to communicate a meaning not explicitly communicated by the word-symbols. The situation does not occur often, but here is an example:

> **Common sense should tell you that when the meaning of your words cannot be mistaken you can dispense with some punctuation marks.**

When a reader hits the word "that," he knows that it is going to introduce a dependent clause, and he would normally expect the next word to be the subject of that clause. But the next word, "when," must also introduce either a dependent clause or a phrase. The two words "that when," coming together, warn him quite clearly that one clause is being interrupted by the insertion of another, and he does not need a pair of commas to reinforce the warning.

Even when writing this kind of sentence, however, most writers of English cannot shake off completely the notion that a pair of commas belongs around a nonessential element that interrupts the normal order of the sentence. Faced with a dilemma, some writers accordingly make a very curious compromise that is effective, even though it is not strictly logical. They omit the first comma of the pair but insert the second.

> **Common sense should tell you that when the meaning of your words cannot be mistaken, you can dispense with some punctuation marks.**

> **Mary noticed how after the first shyness had worn off and the children were beginning to play with one another, the atmosphere in the room became more pleasant.**

> **It was our understanding that since nobody rose to speak against the motion, nobody seriously objected to it.**

These are all clear sentences, though many readers would find them clearer if punctuated with the complete pair of commas. However, most readers understand them, just as they understand another common type of sentence in which the first element in a pair of commas is usually omitted.

> **Helen went off in the direction of the library, and since he had nothing more interesting to do, Jim followed her.**

> **"By this time," said the professor, "the proposition should be clear; but since some of you still look puzzled, I shall repeat my demonstration."**

When a nonessential, interruptive element immediately follows the coordinating conjunction in a compound sentence, it is common practice to omit the first member of the pair of commas. Usually, however, it is perfectly permissible to use the complete pair if you prefer it.

THE COMMA-PLUS-COORDINATING-CONJUNCTION (. . . , and . . .)

The comma-plus-coordinating-conjunction is a *single* mark composed of two symbols, one of which we normally think of as a punctuation symbol and the other as a word-symbol. Before you attempt to understand the meaning of this mark of punctuation, it would be well to remind yourself what a coordinating conjunction is. The word "conjunction" means "that which ties together." There are two kinds: coordinating and subordinating. A *coordinating conjunction* is a little word (usually *and, but, or, nor*) whose sole function in a sentence is to tie together two elements that are completely equal in value and alike in function. In other words, a coordinating conjunction is a link that joins two exactly similar elements into one, making a compound.

For example, you may make a compound out of two single words in the same construction:

> *Jack* and *Jill* went up the hill. (compound subject)
>
> He *laughed* and *jested* all evening. (compound verb)
>
> He built a *tall* and *stately* dome. (compound modifier)

Or you may write compound phrases:

> I saw the breakers *lifting their crests* and *hurling themselves upon the shore.*

Finally, the coordinating conjunction can make a compound of two dependent clauses if they perform the same function in the sentence.

> Mrs. Henderson, *who lives next door* but *who is seldom at home,* is the person you want to see.

But the coordinating conjunction alone cannot join two *independent* clauses without creating a danger of misunderstanding. Let us try to use it this way and see what is likely to happen.

> **Then Ulysses, uttering a deep, warlike cry,
> felled with one blow the terrified Cyclops and
> his bodyguard ran away in fear.**

Yes, you can understand it, perhaps on the second reading. But at first glance it is confusing, because the ordinary English-speaking person expects the "and" to join two elements in the same construction. It looks to him as if you have a compound object; at first glance, he thinks you mean that Ulysses felled both the Cyclops and his bodyguard. When he hits the verb "ran," he has to read the words again to realize that its subject is "bodyguard."

If you write like this, you do not make your meaning as clear as it ought to be, and you put your reader to unnecessary and annoying trouble. The sentence becomes much more clear if you write it this way:

> **Then Ulysses, uttering a deep, warlike cry,
> felled with one blow the terrified Cyclops, and
> his bodyguard ran away in fear.**

The comma-plus-coordinating-conjunction is a mark of punctuation normally used in only one situation: that is, in the middle of a compound sentence. It *means, at this point in the sentence, one independent clause has been completely stated, and the second one is about to begin.*

EXERCISE

In the sentences below, note carefully which conjunctions join only words, phrases, or dependent clauses in the same construction and which ones join independent clauses. Then punctuate accordingly.

1. It is true that she needs to sleep but I still think we should wake her after six hours.

2. Day in and day out the mailman made his rounds and every day Henry's box was left empty.

3. Those who have read the assignment and those who have not will all be required to take the examination.
4. Either you will take the milk bottles to the shop or I shall have to go myself.
5. He walked far out onto the dock and stood there a long time staring at the water.
6. The old woman who never in her life had been the center of so much attention sat staring at the circle of kindly anxious faces for a long moment and then suddenly she burst into tears.
7. When the cat's away the mice will play for the natural instincts will be dominant.
8. Mr. Jackson the newly elected deacon read the first lesson but the second lesson was delivered as usual by old Dr. Brown who chanted in the same ringing tones we had heard for thirty years.

Certain Permissive Uses

This is the one mandatory use of the comma-plus-coordinating-conjunction: at the midpoint of a compound sentence. Here it must be used if the sentence is to be immediately clear.

But in addition to this instance where you *must* use it, there are several situations where you *may* use the comma-plus-coordinating-conjunction if you want to. In looking them over, it would be well to remember a point that has been made several times in this book. Punctuation is not a strait-jacket designed to make you think and write exactly like everybody else; it is a useful instrument that helps you to communicate exactly the shade of meaning you intend. There are occasions where you can use the comma-plus-coordinating-conjunction or refrain from using it, and in doing one or the other you can show your reader more precisely what you mean.

Consider the sentence in which you have only one subject but you want to tell the reader two different things about that subject.

> **Punctuation has undergone a number of changes and improvements since its first appearance and will undergo more.**

> **The first of these problems is very simple and should give you no trouble.**

> **The abbreviation point looks exactly like the punctuational period but in its function is really quite different.**

Here you have in each sentence a single subject followed by a compound predicate, and the coordinating conjunction alone is sufficient to join the two verbs. But these sentences, punctuated in this manner, may seem to you somewhat hard to read. How can you emphasize to your reader that you are telling him two separate and distinct things about each subject? You can of course repeat the subject before the second verb, making a compound sentence and using the comma-plus-coordinating-conjunction to punctuate it.

> **Punctuation has undergone a number of changes and improvements since its first appearance, and it will undergo more.**

> **The first of these problems is very simple, and it should give you no trouble.**

> **The abbreviation point looks exactly like the punctuational period, but in its function it is really quite different.**

But there is a third thing you may do if you wish. If you dislike the effect of the repeated subject, but still want to emphasize that you are describing two separate actions, you can use the comma-plus-coordinating-conjunction very effectively.

> **Punctuation has undergone a number of changes and improvements since its first appearance, and will undergo more.**
>
> **The first of these problems is very simple, and should give you no trouble.**
>
> **The abbreviation point looks exactly like the punctuational period, but in its function is really quite different.**

What you have done, of course, is to write compound sentences with the subject of the second clause understood rather than stated.

This same principle of making a clear distinction between two actions sometimes applies to modifiers, especially if they are long. Here are some examples of dependent clauses that may be joined by the comma-plus-coordinating-conjunction, if you feel that this mark will make your intentions clearer than the conjunction alone would do.

> **Either one is a kind of wedding ring, which tells the reader that here two distinct entities are joined together and made one, and that he must not attempt to put them asunder.**
>
> **If you use the colon, you tell the reader not only that the two parts of your sentence are related, but that they are related in a special way.**

Even in writing compound phrases, you may sometimes find your sentence more clear or your meaning more precise if you use the comma-plus-coordinating-conjunction.

> **Be able to explain every mark of punctuation you have used, and to show how that mark reveals the meaning you wish to convey.**

You may often find this heavier punctuation not necessary, especially when the phrases are short and the sentence is compact.

> **Be able to explain your work and to correct it if it is wrong.**

But the length of the sentence is not the best criterion for determining what punctuation you want to use. If, in the above example, you wish to make it clear that your instructions demand two separate actions, both important, the comma-plus-conjunction will help you.

> **Be able to explain your work, and to correct it if it is wrong.**

Remember that no question of "correctness" is involved in all these examples; they are all correct. Effective punctuation is not a matter of blindly obeying rules. If you find that changing a coordinating conjunction to a comma-plus-conjunction will make your meaning more precise and your sentence more easily comprehensible, by all means make the change.

THE SEMICOLON (;)

If you have understood the meaning of the comma-plus-coordinating-conjunction, you should have no trouble with the semicolon, for it means exactly the same thing. Whenever you wish your reader to understand that you are combining *two independent clauses* into *one compound sentence* because the ideas expressed are actually one idea, you indicate the point at which the two clauses are joined by inserting either the comma-plus-coordinating-conjunction or the semicolon. Take, for example, these two statements:

> **When the war ended, Europe was in a state of chaos.**
>
> *and*
>
> **From one end of the continent to the other, factories were destroyed and people were starving.**

If you wish your reader to understand that these two are separate and distinct ideas, you punctuate them as two separate sentences, using the period and the capital letter to make your intention clear. But if you want him to understand that these two ideas are so closely involved in each other as to form *one* idea, you can write either:

> **When the war ended, Europe was in a state of chaos, and from one end of the continent to the other, factories were destroyed and people were starving.**
>
> *or*
>
> **When the war ended, Europe was in a state of chaos; from one end of the continent to the other, factories were destroyed and people were starving.**

Grammatically, these two sentences have exactly the same meaning. The difference is purely a rhetorical one. You may use the comma-plus-coordinating-conjunction because it makes your sentence read a little more smoothly, or you may use the semicolon to get a more crisp effect. But your meaning is the same.

Suppose a person comes into a room full of people and asks, "Where are Henry and Peter?" One of the group in the room might answer:

> **Henry has gone down to the beach. Peter is in the next room telephoning.**

The person who gives this answer, punctuated in this way, sees no connection between the two actions he has described. He thinks of them as two completely different actions, probably because his mind has interpreted the question as two questions ("Where is Henry?" and "Where is Peter?") since he knew in advance that the two had gone off in different directions on different errands.

But another person in the same room might just as sensibly answer:

> **Henry has gone down to the beach, and Peter is in the next room telephoning.**

This person thinks differently from the one whose answer was given in the preceding paragraph. To him, the question is *one*, a compound. He therefore gives one compound answer. He thinks of it not so much as a description of two actions but as a statement which supplies the one piece of information asked for: "Where are these two people?" He could just as well have said:

> **Henry has gone down to the beach; Peter is in the next room telephoning.**

Why didn't he? Because he was not writing, but speaking aloud, and we have no oral inflection in ordinary conversational speech to indicate the kind of jointure which a written semicolon indicates.

Notice that each of these three methods of punctuating the same two clauses (and there is yet a fourth possible way, which we shall take up in good time) is perfectly clear and perfectly correct. No one can possibly say that one way is "right" and the others "wrong"; the question of correctness depends entirely on what meaning the writer or speaker wishes to communicate. So long as you use each mark of punctuation in its accepted meaning, your reader will understand what you write, no matter how much your ideas and your way of thinking may differ from his own. Of course you cannot arbitrarily *change* the meaning of any mark. You cannot decide that for you a period is going to mean "here a slight element is omitted" or that a question mark is going to mean "pause slightly at this point." If you want to be understood, you cannot write things like this:

the weaRy: man, st /opped working and — sat. Down

You may insist that in some wonderful new system which you have invented each of the idiosyncrasies in that line has some definite and important meaning, but your reader will simply conclude (and quite rightly) that you are either mentally unbalanced or insufferably egotistical. Freedom in the use of punctuation marks is like any other freedom, in that it rests upon the recognition and utilization of necessity. The necessity involved here is the socially recognized meaning of each mark.

In written English, the comma-plus-conjunction has the same meaning as the semicolon. Either one is a kind of wedding ring, which tells the reader that here two distinct entities are joined together and made one, and that he must not attempt to put them asunder.

EXERCISE

After you have punctuated the various sentences in the following exercise, be sure that you can justify your punctuation in each instance by explaining clearly what meaning you wish the reader to understand and what rhetorical effect you wish to suggest. You may use the comma-plus-coordinating conjunction or the semicolon, or write two separate sentences, depending on what you mean.

1. He decided to leave early therefore he set the alarm but of course he slept right through it.
2. Whenever the students play there are cheers and catcalls when the old gentlemen play there is a dignified silence.
3. If the snow continues the west will be isolated wit')ut hope of new supplies by road transport the town will have to rely on air drop.
4. We're with you whatever happens win lose or draw you can do no wrong.
5. There was little to be done they could thank their stars they were alive.
6. They failed to define their terms therefore their argument arour ;d heat but no light.
7. We cannot hope to win I admit with so little preparation nevertheless we have no choice but to try.

Two Important Variations

There is one situation in which, in order to make the meaning as clear as possible to the reader, these two marks of punctuation (semicolon and comma-plus-coordinating conjunction) are frequently combined. Consider the following compound sentence:

> **The musicians began to beat loudly upon a wierd collection of instruments, including a drum made of elephant hide, a hollowed log, and a kind of tambourine, and a beautiful, dark-skinned girl, after the noise had been going on for several minutes, rose swiftly and began to perform an intricate dance.**

Here the *comma and* that immediately follows the word "tambourine" is the wedding ring, marking the point at which the two independent clauses are joined to compose one sentence. But the sentence is a little confusing to the reader because each of the major clauses contains within itself a good bit of interior punctuation. For one thing, the first clause contains a pair of commas around the phrase "including a . . . of tambourine." In addition, this first clause contains two single commas, and the second of these (after "log") is followed by an "and" which has been inserted for rhetorical effect. A hasty reader, having noticed that, might read right on through the central *comma and,* mistaking it for another single comma before the last element in a series, and get the impression that the beautiful girl also received a beating. In order to avoid this kind of confusion, you can of course indicate the central juncture of the sentence by using a semicolon instead of the comma-plus-coordinating conjunction. But that will not give you the same smooth rhetorical effect, melting one action into the other, as it were. Therefore, you can in such a situation perform a sort of "double wedding ring" ceremony by combining the two marks into one, making a *semicolon-plus-coordinating-conjunction.* For complete clearness of meaning, you can write:

> **The musicians began to beat loudly upon a weird collection of instruments, including a drum made of elephant hide, a hollowed log, and a kind of tambourine; and a beautiful, dark-skinned girl, after the noise had been going on for several minutes, rose swiftly and began to perform an intricate dance.**

The semicolon is a very noticeable mark; used thus, it shows your reader at a glance the major junction point of your sentence.

A second important variation occurs when a single comma is arbitrarily raised to a semicolon in the interests of complete clarity. You will occasionally write a sentence in which you have a series of long and complicated elements, in at least some of which there is interior punctuation. In such a sentence, if you use the single comma to indicate the omission of conjunctions between the elements in the series, you may succeed in confusing your reader.

> **During the course of one hour's journey through the country, the explorer saw fourteen hyenas, a jaguar, which is a kind of tiger, a flock of strange waterfowl, some with brilliant plumage and some as soberly gray as the quietest, most demure of our farmyard ducks, and three herds of wild elephants.**

In such a sentence, you will do your reader a service if you arbitrarily change the single commas which separate the elements in series to semicolons. The more noticeable mark will show him instantly how many elements are in the series and what are the outside limits of each.

> **During the course of one hour's journey through the country, the explorer saw fourteen hyenas; a jaguar, which is a kind of tiger; a flock of strange waterfowl, some with brilliant plumage and some as soberly gray as the quietest, most demure of our farmyard ducks; and three herds of wild elephants.**

EXERCISE

1. It is amazing how quickly we adapted ourselves to army life: to march and to groan and sing at once to dig and to fill in what we dug to get up with a bugle and without time to dress to fall out completely awake to obey and to goldbrick with equal insouciance.

2. The airplane is a wonderful instrument of cooperating contradictions its speed is its safety its height its money in the bank its turn is made with both rudder and stick the more stick the less rudder when you lose speed you aim for the

ground and recover flaps must be used for takeoff and mustn't be forgotten when you want to land or have to.

3. When I stop to consider everything that grows seems to have its moment of mystery every manifestation of nature conspires to fill us with awe but we are soon brought down to earth by its most trivial denizens a flea a mosquito a gnat which have not read the poets will perform their workaday interruptions.

THE COLON (:)

At the beginning of the section on the semicolon, you were asked to observe that two statements, when punctuated as separate sentences, indicate that the writer considers them to express two separate and complete thoughts.

> When the war ended, Europe was in a state of chaos. From one end of the continent to the other, factories were destroyed and people were starving.

You also noticed that if the writer thinks of the two statements as in reality one, he can explain his meaning clearly to the reader by using either the comma-plus-coordinating-conjunction or the semicolon.

There is yet a third possible meaning which the reader may wish to communicate, and he has available for the purpose another mark of punctuation.

> When the war ended, Europe was in a state of chaos: from one end of the continent to the other, factories were destroyed and people were starving.

What change in meaning has been imparted to the sentence? In other words, what does the colon mean? Perhaps some further examples will give you the answer.

Johnny behaved very badly: he shrieked, made hideous faces, and threw his pudding upon the floor.

Mrs. James found herself in a quandary: she could neither pay for the unwanted goods nor return them to the shop.

Please remember to bring me four articles: a comb, a razor, a toothbrush, and a cake of soap.

If you will look over these sentences, you will notice that each contains first a complete statement, an independent clause. At the end of this clause appears the colon. Then comes, what? Look at the three sentences again, and you will see that in each the words following the colon give the reader a *fuller explanation* of something said in the first clause. "He shrieked . . ." explains more fully what the writer means by saying that Johnny behaved badly. In the second example, the words following the colon explain more fully the quandary of Mrs. James. In the last, they explain more precisely what four articles are wanted. Therefore we can say that *the colon means that the words which follow immediately will give a fuller explanation of what has just been stated.*

There are several points about this mark and its usage which you should note especially. In the first place, check back to the sentence about the state of Europe and observe that when it is punctuated with the colon it has a different meaning from the one it conveys when punctuated with another mark. If you use the colon, you tell the reader not only that the two parts of your sentence are related, but that they are related in a special way, that is, that the second is a fuller explanation of the first. This re-emphasizes the point that punctuation exists to enable you to write clearly and effectively what *you* mean.

The second thing to notice about the colon is that most commonly it comes at the end of a complete statement that could stand alone as a sentence. This is not always literally true, of course. You will find occasions for using the colon at the end of what is technically an incompleted clause.

> **The normal order of an English sentence is always: subject with its modifiers, verb with its modifiers, and object or verb complement with its modifiers.**

> **The sentence will become clearer to the reader if you write: "The entire city (pop. 47,000 in 1940) was placed under martial law."**

In the first of these examples, the element before the colon lacks a verb complement; in the second, a modifying clause lacks an object. But in both of them, the missing elements are *understood,* although not stated. What the writer means is perfectly clear.

> **The normal order of an English sentence is always *this:* subject with its modifiers, verb with its modifiers, and object or verb complement with its modifiers.**

> **The sentence will become clearer to the reader if you write *some such statement as the following:* "The entire city (pop. 47,000 in 1940) was placed under martial law."**

In all such instances, the colon means that what is to follow will explain more fully what has gone before.

Be particularly careful to avoid the common error of using a colon when it is not needed.

> **I asked him to buy such items as: nails, hammer, saw, and screwdriver.**

**I asked him to buy several items, such as:
nails, hammer, saw, and screwdriver.**

The colons here are useless and distracting. The phrase
"such as" communicates to the reader perfectly clearly
that what is to follow will explain the word "items," and
if you put in a colon you are only saying the same thing
twice. Remember that a mark of punctuation is a conventional symbol used to communicate a meaning *not
explicitly communicated by the word-symbols.* Wherever you
have a choice between a word-symbol and a punctua-
tion-symbol that means exactly the same thing, use
whichever you please, but not both. Write either

**I asked him to buy several items, such as
nails, hammer, saw, and screwdriver.**

or

**I asked him to buy several items: nails, ham-
mer, saw, and screwdriver.**

Finally, there is one rather formal convention
in English writing which involves the use of a colon. It
is customary to place a colon after the salutation at the
beginning of a formal letter or a formal speech.

Dear Sir:

Dear Mr. President:

Mr. Chairman, ladies and gentlemen:

This convention has nothing to do with the punctuation
of ordinary prose or verse. In the strict sense of the
word, it is not a mark of punctuation at all, but merely
a conventional flourish we have got into the habit of
making. But it would be wise for you to take note of it,
and to use it when addressing anyone with whom you
wish to preserve the courtesies of formal good man-
ners.

1. I never heard the likes babies squalling radio blaring pots clashing and the older children shouting to make themselves heard and I hope never to hear such a racket again.

2. The conductor announced a rather unimaginative program Brahms Tchaikowsky and Franck.

3. The teacher's announcement of the marks aroused a groan no A's 3 B's 4 C's and the rest F's.

4. Miss Gray take the following letter Dear Dr. Abernethy whenever you can you are welcome to come visit our school especially the gymnasium and the dining room and the quadrangle and the theater are particularly attractive.

5. Whoever you are this caution is directed toward you a house cannot stand and live half free and half terrorized.

5
Rarely Needed Interior Marks

THE SINGLE DASH (—)

Dashes have recently become the most trouble-some marks of punctuation in English writing. Not long ago, they were very rarely used. If they were properly understood, they would be just as rare today. But a while back they suddenly became a fad, and like most fads they have been adopted with gusto by all sorts of people. Today many writers sprinkle dashes merrily over their pages without the slightest regard for their meaning and indeed with no apparent awareness that they have a meaning. Since they are as annoying to a sensitive reader as a multiplicity of exclamation points, it behooves you to understand them and to use them with moderation.

In the first place, you should notice carefully that there are two separate and distinct marks: the single dash and the pair of dashes. Just as the pair of commas conveys a totally different meaning from that indicated by the single comma, so the single dash is a totally different mark of punctuation from the pair of dashes (which we will discuss on p. 69). Like all the others, it conveys a definite meaning, but one which you will need to express very, very rarely.

The easiest way to understand the single dash is to associate it with the colon. You remember that the colon means that what follows will explain more fully what has just been said.

> **Everything conspired to make it a delightful picnic: perfect weather, lots of good food, and a company of congenial people.**

Once in a great while you might wish to turn such a sentence around and give the explanation *first,* before the summarizing statement. If you should, the single dash is the only mark that will show your intention to the reader clearly.

> **Perfect weather, lots of good food, and a company of congenial people — everything conspired to make it a delightful picnic.**

This kind of sentence presents the sole occasion for using the single dash. *The single dash means, the preceding elements in this sentence explain more fully the statement now to be made.*

Many people seem to be vaguely aware that the single dash is in some way related in meaning to the colon. The trouble is that they apparently think it means the same thing. Hence the most common error made in connection with the single dash is the use of it in place of the colon. In almost any magazine or newspaper you pick up, you will find punctuation like this:

> **There are two kinds of frozen food — quick-frozen and slow-frozen.**

Avoid this error by fixing firmly in your mind the fact that the single dash is exactly opposite in meaning to the colon.

Here are some more examples of the only type

of sentence in which the intended meaning can be expressed by the single dash.

> James, Dorothy, Henry, David, and Elizabeth — these five nominees will please retire while we vote on them.

> Two dozen eggs, a loaf of bread, a head of lettuce, and two pounds of cheese — is that all you wanted?

> But the girl is only four feet six inches tall — she could not have done it.

A rather unusual example. It would normally be stated the other way around, thus: "But the girl could not have done it: she is only four feet six inches tall." However, since the fuller explanation is placed first, the single dash is the only mark which indicates the proper meaning.

You have on several occasions observed that the same group of words, punctuated differently, may communicate different meanings. Here is an example which will show you again how vital the punctuation marks are. Take one of the sentences that was used to demonstrate the single comma:

> We demand an end to tyranny, a breaking of bonds we have endured too long.

Punctuated thus, the sentence means that we demand two things: "an end" and "a breaking." We have expressed our meaning by making a compound object of the verb, "demand."

You have noticed that we get a different meaning if we use the colon.

> We demand an end to tyranny: a breaking of bonds we have endured too long.

Now we are demanding only one thing, "an end to tyranny." After stating the demand, we explain more specifically what we mean by that phrase.

But there is a third possible meaning in these words.

We demand an end to tyranny — a breaking of bonds we have endured too long.

This is an unusual sentence, granted. But it does communicate a meaning, although a rather uncommon one. We are demanding one thing, "a breaking of bonds," but we are so angry and excited that we blurt out first an explanation of what this breaking would mean to us, namely, an end to tyranny.

EXERCISE

1. Man or mouse well what are you make up your mind.
2. Money clothes and boy friends is that all that's ever on your mind?
3. Friend or foe speak up man.
4. There's no end to human misery birth shock the terrors of childhood the disappointments of youth these we must all suffer and try to fit ourselves into what we know we are if we would achieve a happy world.
5. And don't expect me to come to your rescue whatever you've done and I expect the worst borrowing beyond your allowance teasing the girls and striking out with two men on I must start letting nature take its course.
6. The war to end wars who takes that phrase seriously any more?
7. Liberty or death that was the choice Patrick Henry dramatically made because the occasion called for dramatic action the young hillsman did not miss his opportunity.

The pair of dashes (see pp. 69–73) is an entirely different mark from the single dash. It can best be understood after you have studied the parentheses.

Do Not Confuse the Single Dash with the Hyphen

The hyphen is not a mark of punctuation. It is a small symbol, less than half as long as the single dash, used in *spelling*. We use it to join two or more words into one compound word.

a two-year-old child   **forty-seven**

It is also used, as you know, at the end of a line of print when a word is broken between syllables. There seems no good reason why anybody should confuse it with the single dash, a much larger symbol and one which is used only for the punctuation of one rare kind of sentence, but a good many people do. Perhaps the cause may lie in the fact that the modern typewriter, although it has a key for the hyphen, has none for the dash. If you are typing, the only way you can indicate a dash clearly is by striking the hyphen key twice.

THE PARENTHESES

Simple sentences in English normally need little, if any, interior punctuation. The grammatical function of each word is made clear by its position, and with every word exactly where the reader expects it to be the thought flows smoothly from the capital letter to the end mark without the reader's needing any punctuation to clarify it.

But the average writer of English composes comparatively few simple sentences. Sometimes he combines two simple sentences into one, and uses either the semicolon or the comma-plus-conjunction to show the reader where the two are joined. More often, he makes what are called "complex" sentences, in which he interrupts or changes the normal order of the simple sentence by putting in some word or group of words which, though it gives some additional meaning to the sentence, is not essential to the grammatical structure. You have discovered (on p. 22) that you can usually make such sentences easily readable and clear to your reader by enclosing the slightly interruptive element within a pair of commas, "setting it off" visually from the other words. In ninety-nine complex sentences out of a hundred, that small mark of punctuation is sufficient to give the reader all the notice he needs that the word-order is not exactly as he expects.

But very occasionally you may need to introduce into a sentence an element that interrupts the grammatical structure and the flow of the thought more seriously, even perhaps violently. To indicate such more unexpected breaks, you need larger, heavier, more noticeable marks than the pair of commas. The first to be considered is the parentheses.

In discussing the pair of commas, we sometimes described the interruptive element as "parenthetical." This usage suggests that the parentheses are a mark of punctuation closely related in meaning to the pair of commas. The two marks are, as a matter of fact, quite similar; the difference is simply one of degree.

The entire city, which by 1940 had a population of 47,000, was placed under martial law.

The nonessential element in this sentence undoubtedly interrupts the normal order of the words. Yet the interruption is not particularly disturbing. The fact that it is stated as a relative clause indicates its definite relationship to the rest of the sentence. So long as the reader has been warned by the pair of commas that the normal, expected order has been changed, he can read the sentence quickly and easily and with full understanding of its meaning.

But let us see what happens if we use the pair of commas around a differently constructed element.

> The entire city, pop. 47,000 in 1940, was placed under martial law.

Here the break is much more abrupt. The interpolated element seems to have little, if any, grammatical relationship to the rest of the sentence. The reader will understand your statement more easily and more clearly if you write:

> The entire city (pop. 47,000 in 1940) was placed under martial law.

From this example, we can determine *the meaning of the parentheses: the normal order of the sentence is here changed by the insertion of a nonessential element so phrased that it shows little, if any, grammatical relationship to the rest of the sentence.*

Here are two further examples to illustrate the meaning and effectiveness of the parentheses.

> In a whole series of decisions (see especially *State of Arizona* v. *Mead* and *Cowan* v. *Cowan,* xii, 59 and 427), the courts have upheld the right of the individual to appeal from a judgment of this sort.

> It is true that there are a few occasions (mark that word "few") on which such dress is appropriate

In examples like these, the lack of grammatical relationship between the interpolated elements and the rest of the sentence is very clear. But there are many sentences in which the degree of clear relationship presents something of a problem. Which of the two marks of punctuation, for example, is better in the following sentence?

> **She said that a certain Henry Cummings, that person being a relative of the deceased, should be consulted.**
>
> *or*
>
> **She said that a certain Henry Cummings (that person being a relative of the deceased) should be consulted.**

Some writers contend that it is a matter of one's personal taste. But whose taste? The writer's or the reader's? You will be wiser to establish your procedure on a solider basis. Regardless of what your personal taste or that of your reader may be, your reader will receive a meaning from every symbol you employ. The only sensible way to decide which mark of punctuation to use in this sentence is to determine which of two slightly different meanings you wish to convey. If you wish to warn your reader that a nonessential, interruptive element is so phrased that he will have difficulty in perceiving its grammatical relationship to the rest of your sentence, enclose it within parentheses. If you wish him to understand that the grammatical relationship is there and clearly observable, use the pair of commas.

Better still, do not write ambiguous sentences and then try to make them clear by punctuation. The best thing to do with the sentence about Henry Cummings would be to rephrase it so that the word-symbols will carry the major burden of the communication.

> **She said that a certain Henry Cummings, a relative of the deceased, should be consulted.**
>
> *or*

> She said that a certain Henry Cummings
> should be consulted, since he was a relative
> of the deceased.

In the first of these, "she" is suggesting that Cummings should be consulted in his own right, and is merely adding the information that he is related to the dead person. In the second, "she" suggests that Cummings should be consulted *because of* that relationship. Decide which you mean, and write it.

Incidentally, it might be well to notice that occasionally a mark of punctuation itself is inserted into a smoothly constructed sentence as an interruptive element. The marks so used are the exclamation point and the question mark, each of which carries with it the suggestion of a particular tone of voice or intellectual or emotional attitude. If you wish to raise a doubt in your reader's mind about some detail in your sentence, you can do so by inserting a question mark enclosed within parentheses. A suggestion of shock, surprise, sardonic distaste, or some other sharp emotion on the part of the writer is conveyed by an exclamation point within the parentheses.

> This bulletin announces that there are more
> than half a million families (?) who employ at
> least one full-time servant.

> The Fascist protested that it was love of man-
> kind (!) that made him desire to murder all
> Jews, Negroes, trade-union members, ho-
> mosexuals, Communists, Socialists, athi-
> ests, and many kinds of Christians.

You should use this kind of thing sparingly, however. It is much loved by "gushy" writers, and overuse of it makes any writer appear slightly ridiculous. It would be wise to observe that by careful writing you can create any kind of intellectual or emotional response you want, without leaning on the crutch of interpolated exclamation points and question marks. If you feel that you must use them, put them inside parentheses. But it would be better to learn to write effectively without them.

A final remark needs to be made about the parentheses. You have observed that when one part of the pair of commas coincides in position with another mark of punctuation, it is absorbed by a more emphatic mark (capital letter, period, semicolon, or colon) and absorbs a less emphatic one (single comma). This is not true of the parentheses, as you can see illustrated in the preceding sentence, where the parenthesis in the final position is followed by the period. The parentheses enclose the parenthetical element, but it is still necessary to punctuate the end of the sentence. Notice that the other mark of punctuation always stands outside the parenthesis. The only exceptions to this are found when an entire sentence or group of sentences is considered parenthetical or when the interpolated matter contains quotation marks; in either of these situations, the parentheses go outside, enclosing the entire interpolation, which is punctuated as it normally would be.

EXERCISE

1. wherever he is and I'm not sure he's alive at all he'll have to revisit the scene of his crime and then we'll have our chance after all these years to nab the culprit but whatever he's done and he's done plenty we shall try to forgive but forget never

2. although this point has raised much controversy *cf*. Miller *op. cit.* p. 39 there is no doubt that the author presents his material with masterly scholarship *v*. p. 84

3. I don't think you can really be so cruel as to recommend drowning them if that's what I understood you to say

4. at this time of year and isn't it a lovely day you can expect to see at least a dozen kinds of birds all busy making nests or stealing them if the tradition about the cuckoo has any basis in fact

5. the only thing left is to attack before dawn or wouldn't you agree colonel

6. the coach threw in all his reserves all three of them

7. if you or any of your accomplices are found skulking around here again there will be the dickens to pay plus a nice fat fine

THE PAIR OF DASHES (— . . . —)

This mark has lately been more widely over-used and misused even than the single dash. In certain quarters it has become so ubiquitous that it is difficult to find a paragraph in which at least one pair of dashes is not wholly or partially visible. Journalists, whose job it is to provide a day-by-day record of the state of the world in their time, seem to be the principal offenders, and it may be that they have been led into their offense by a sincere effort to communicate something of the near-hysteria of mankind in this unhappy century. For the primary implication of the pair of dashes is a lack of rational processes of thought.

This statement may offend many perfectly sane people who have become addicted to the pair of dashes without ever realizing the sinister implications of their addiction. Nevertheless, we cannot ignore the fact that when we use any mark of punctuation we communicate a meaning to the reader, whether we intended to do so or not. And *the pair of dashes means that the enclosed element interrupts the formal flow of the thought so violently and with such complete disregard for rational relationships that there is no other way it can be got into the sentence at all.*

Of course, when the average devotee of the pair

of dashes uses this very heavy mark of punctuation, he does not intend to convey this meaning. He actually has quite different intentions when he writes sentences like the following:

> **Every cabin has its stack of peat — unquestionably the best in Ireland — cut from the family's patch of bog.**

> *or*

> **The Navy began testing them at some of its larger establishments — among them the Great Lakes Naval Training Station — before adopting them for general use.**

You can cull examples like these from any newspaper or magazine you may pick up. If you collect and examine enough of them, you will discover that in most of them the meaning intended by the writer would be better expressed either by completely recast sentences or by the use of another, less obtrusive mark of punctuation, such as the pair of commas or the parentheses. The careful writer should choose the one that most nearly suggests the degree of interruption he intends, and he should remember that since the pair of dashes indicates a really violent break, it should be reserved for enclosing interruptive elements which do real violence to the syntax and the flow of thought.

If you are recording the speech of an hysterical person, for example, you will find it necessary to use many pairs of dashes, for one of the usual symptoms of hysteria is an inability to think in any rational order. The speeches of a demagogue are often heavily interlarded with dashes, for they are usually designed not to communicate any coherent argument but simply to work the listeners into an irrational frenzy. For such a diabolical purpose, violent and illogical outbursts are more effective than clear, rationally organized prose.

Sometimes a very careful, logical thinker will use the pair of dashes where another equally careful writer might use the parentheses.

> **The growing pressure of population, however — London rose from around 100,000 at the beginning of Elizabeth's reign to double that number under her successor — had long since pushed some of the inhabitants outside the ancient walls.**

Here there is no emotional violence, no melodrama. The minds of both writer and reader are perfectly calm and rational. But to the writer it seems that the break in syntax is as violent as it could be. Nothing, he thinks, could come nearer to disrupting the syntax of his sentence than the intrusion into it of another complete sentence, and a long sentence at that. Therefore he tries to warn the reader of this long "digression" which intervenes between his subject and its verb. The pair of dashes is the most effective mark at his disposal; it glares like the red traffic light before a temporary one-way stretch on a highway, telling the motorist to wait until the on-coming traffic has passed before proceeding on his way.

There is another kind of grammatically interruptive element which all writers enclose within a pair of dashes. You will remember that a colon tells the reader that a completed statement is to be followed by elements which will explain the statement more fully.

> **I asked him to buy several items: nails, hammer, saw, and screwdriver.**

But if such an element is placed within a sentence where it disrupts the normal order, it seems to most readers to interrupt the flow of thought quite seriously. It is therefore enclosed within a pair of dashes.

> I asked him to buy several items — nails, hammer, saw, and screwdriver — at the ironmonger's shop.

In other words, an explanatory list thrust between essential elements that belong together, seems as violent an intrusion as a complete sentence.

On very rare occasions, and normally only when you are writing dialogue, you may find that a sentence is interrupted so violently that it is never completed. In this situation, the pair of dashes is never completed, either; the reader sees only the first part of the punctuation mark.

> "But I never said that your father was — "
> "Yes, you did!" she cried out bitterly, pressing her hands over her ears to blot out the dreadful word she hoped she had prevented him from uttering.

From these examples, you can see that there is a time and place for everything, even for so dramatic a mark as the pair of dashes. But you will also have observed that there are very few occasions that call for it. Over-used, it makes a writer appear hysterical.

EXERCISE

Some of these sentences need the pair of dashes and some need other punctuation marks, or to be rewritten. Decide what meaning you want to express and write and punctuate accordingly.

1. If you insist on acting this way gosh I wish I had had the bringing up of you there's no knowing where you'll end in a ditch most likely dead drunk

2. The hue and cry that arose no matter how absurd and hysterical was the result of a carefully planned heightening of tension.

3. Whenever I brought up the subject of a raise and I was not as bashful then as I seem to be now he started telling me his baby's latest tricks or his latest off-color joke anything to change the subject.

4. The New York celebrity who is Manhattan-born how you gonna keep 'em down on the farm is as rare as the champion baseball player who was born in the town he represents.

5. If we had world enough and time oh there's no use thinking about it. But the world is what it is and who ever had time for one umpteenth of what he wanted to do assuming that we ever really know what we want.

6

Punctuation of Quoted Matter

THE QUOTATION MARKS

Up to this point we have been discussing the marks of punctuation you will need within your sentences in order to make clear to your reader exactly what your own word-symbols mean. Now we shall consider briefly the familiar marks you will employ when you quote the words of someone else. Like the capital letter and the end-of-sentence marks, they are probably so well known to you that you can define them yourself. *The element enclosed within the quotation marks comprises the exact words of some other writer or speaker.*

> Patrick Henry said, "Give me liberty or give me death."
>
> The Holy Roman Empire was, as some wit once remarked, "neither holy, nor Roman, nor an empire."
>
> "Is there anybody there?" said the Traveller,
> Knocking on the moonlit door,
> And his horse in the silence champed the grasses
> Of the forest's ferny floor.

> The German expression is "butterfly weeks," a delightfully giddy term, far more delicate and witty in its connotation than our sentimental "honeymoon."

In the last of these examples, notice that the author is quoting the exact words of a whole group of people rather than of one individual. Yet this is still a direct quotation. The same principle applies to any situation in which one calls attention to a particular word *as a word*, as illustrated in the next two examples, for in such a situation the author is quoting either himself or the whole English-speaking population.

> I ask you to note particularly that "possibly," for I would not have you believe that I am being dogmatic.

> "Democracy" is used very carelessly by this editor, who seems to equate it with the private ownership of farms, factories, resources, and communications.

Slang words, when they are used in formal writing, are put inside quotation marks; the theory is that the writer would not use such words himself but is merely quoting people who do.

> If Harry can protect himself against the allurements of "punk," he may eventually make himself a good pianist.

Of course you will also find the quotation marks used as a substitute for some such phrase as "what might be called" or "as the saying goes." Here, again, the element inside the marks is quoted from those who use it.

> These "shorthand" symbols are called abbreviation points.

> More people have been defeated by the "rules
> of punctuation" than have ever been helped
> by them.

There is one pure convention in the use of
quotation marks that you should notice. *It is customary
to put quotation marks around the title of any single part or
section of a bound volume:* a single poem, a short story, a
chapter, an article, etc.

> You will find Pope's "The Rape of the Lock"
> in any good edition of his work.

> The third chapter, "How the Brain Works,"
> contains the essence of the whole book.

> "The Discontented Grass Plant" is one of the
> stories in *A Harvest of World Folk Tales.*

Notice that the title of a bound volume is printed in
italics. For an explanation of how to indicate this in
handwriting or typewriting, see the section on "Underscoring" in this book, p. 86.

The single quotation marks are also familiar.
As you know, they mean that the element they enclose
is a direct quotation which is itself embedded in another
direct quotation.

> "Julius Caesar," continued the speaker, "was
> always ready to boast, 'I came; I saw; I con-
> quered', whenever his toops had pillaged
> some defenseless collection of primitive huts
> and massacred their inhabitants."

> "We are guilty of gross misuse of language,"
> said Dr. Henderson, "when we employ the
> word 'nice' as a synonym for anything from
> 'sharp' to 'pretty' or 'pleasant'."

An Important Convention in Printing

The only question that is likely to arise concerning quotation marks is a question not of meaning but of usage, that is, the way in which printers handle them. You will have understood that the quotation marks, if they are to communicate their meaning clearly, should enclose only the matter that is quoted. You will also have noticed that when a quotation mark comes next to any other mark of punctuation, neither one absorbs the other; they are both used. It would seem, then, that any mark immediately preceding or following the quoted matter should be placed outside the quotation marks, and it usually is.

> After all, "inevitable" is a very strong word.
>
> Bring me some of those "what-you-may-call-its": those things you use to fix your hair.
>
> Shakespeare often glorifies such "villains"; it is one of the most noticeable facts about his work.
>
> Who was it said, "We have met the enemy and they are ours"?

This sensible practice is universally followed by writers and printers alike with respect to all marks of punctuation when they *precede* the quoted matter, as you can see in the first and last of the examples above. It is also universally followed when a colon, semicolon, question mark, parenthesis, bracket, exclamation point, or dash *follows* the quoted matter. But if you look into almost any printed book (including this one you are reading), you will find a noticeable exception to this general practice.

When a quotation should be followed in the sentence by a *period*, or by any mark that contains the *comma-symbol* (the single comma, the pair of commas, or the comma-plus-coordinating-conjunction), most printers will set this very small mark (. *or* ,) *inside* the final element of the quotation marks, even if this practice splits apart the comma-plus-coordinating-conjunction symbol. Here are some common examples of the printers' methods.

> **"Inevitable," like many other expressions of finality, is too strong to be used here.**

> **Bring me some of those "what-you-may-call-its."**

> **Shakespeare often glorifies such "villains," but that is no reason why you should do so.**

This practice of the printers may puzzle you, but it need concern you only if you are preparing a manuscript for printed publication. In that event, it will be wise to follow the advice you will find in the standard books on manuscript style. All of these will explain to you that printers always place periods and commas *inside* end-quotation marks, and that they do this for purely aesthetic reasons, regardless of how the writer may have written it and regardless of the logic of the sentence they are setting up in type.

> **Typographical usage dictates that the comma be inside the [quotation] marks though logically it often seems not to belong there.**
> **— Strunk and White: *Elements of Style***

> **The placing of quotation marks in connection with any other punctuation follows the standard procedures instituted by printers for the sake of the physical appearance of the page. Periods and commas are always placed inside end-quotation marks.**
> **— Hopper and Gale: *Essentials of English***

This practice of the printers is a firmly established convention, which editors, copy readers, and printers are not likely to change. Therefore, if you intend what you write to be published, you may as well, whenever you find a period or one of the comma-symbols following the final member of a pair of quotation marks, put it inside. But remember that you can only make your own writing completely clear by putting all other marks of punctuation where they logically belong.

EXERCISE

1. the ancient folk were wise, and had an old saw for every occasion, but we need wisdom too to choose between conflicting advice a stitch in time saves nine is not quite the same as look before you leap.

2. say it this way how now brown cow

3. you can't mean it she panted I can't can't I he replied with a melodramatic sneer then take a look at this

4. I read your last article color television is here to stay in *Everyman's* magazine and I wish I had your faith in science but wait and see is my motto

5. I heard you say there's little in coleridge beyond kubla khan and the ancient mariner but I must ask you what about christabel and the volume called biographia literaria

6. where will all this soul-searching lead the lecturer asked but did he ask where will a civilization go without soul-searching

THE BRACKETS

The parentheses and brackets are similar in meaning: they both indicate a more serious interruption of the normal order than is indicated by the pair of commas. The difference between them is, again, one of degree. The brackets are more noticeable, and as such they are used to call the reader's attention to a more unexpected break in the normal order. In ordinary writing, they are very seldom needed, but you will find a few rather uncommon situations in which no other mark will so clearly communicate your meaning.

Occasionally, in quoting material from some other writer or speaker, you may wish to insert into the quotation some remark of your own. If you used the parentheses, your reader would think that the element was a parenthetical comment made by the original author of the material you are quoting. The only mark which will serve your purpose is a pair of brackets.

> **According to the stenographic record, the Representative became very angry. "If the gentleman would spend some time in my part of the country," he shouted, "he would find that people of Niles and Hampton [small towns in the speaker's district] look with contempt upon his proposals!"**

The meaning of this very heavy mark is this: *the element enclosed within the pair of brackets is an explanatory remark inserted into the quotation by the quoter.*

Normally, of course, you must not alter quoted material in any way, in fairness to the author whom you are quoting. You will find even fewer occasions for using the brackets in sentences that contain only your own words. For example, if you write one interruptive element inside another, doubly quoting yourself, as it were, your reader will need unmistakeable punctuation. Two sets of parentheses, one inside the other, can be very confusing. It is therefore customary to change the inner set to a pair of brackets.

> **The entire city (pop. in 1940 [see census figures in *The World Almanac*] 14,000) was put under martial law.**

Such a sentence is awkward and offensive, and should be rewritten. But if you should ever write one interruptive element inside another, brackets will at least warn the reader that something very odd has happened to the word order he expects, and he will need to pause and think it out carefully.

You may possibly be puzzled by one particular remark that you will sometimes see in brackets. This is the little comment, *"sic!"* It is a Latin word meaning "thus it stands," and the exclamation point which usually accompanies it indicates that the writer is just as astonished to find it there as the reader is. Its use is generally restricted to careful scholars who, when they find an obvious error in some passage they wish to quote, reproduce the error exactly as it stands in the original but call attention to the fact that they know it is an error by inserting *"sic!"* immediately after it. Some printers enclose this interruptive element in parentheses; most use brackets.

> **Mr. Jones writes, "Regardless of the fact that he killed her, it is evident that Othello was very much in love with Juliet *[sic!]* or he would never have married her."**

THE THREE DOTS (. . .)

Sometimes the normal order of a sentence is broken not by an interruptive element but simply by an omission. No violence is indicated; the writer simply leaves something out. For example, if you are quoting a passage in which certain words, phrases, or whole sentences are not necessary to the point you wish to make, it is perfectly permissible to include in your quotation only those parts your reader needs to follow your thought. But in fairness to the original author of the material you are quoting, you should make clear to your reader what you are doing. You can indicate your omission by using the three dots.

> **The question that bothered Hamlet was, as he said, "whether 'tis nobler in the mind to suffer . . . or to take arms."**

Here we have omitted seven words from the familiar passage and we have told the reader that we are omitting them by using *the three dots*. This mark therefore means that *at this point certain elements are omitted from the original quotation* which are not essential to the purpose at hand.

Another situation involving the same essential meaning occurs when you are quoting a speaker who starts a sentence and lets it trail off without completing it.

> **"Well, I don't know about that," he murmured, hesitating as if groping for words to express his bewilderment. "There are so many problems, so many . . ." His voice died away, but his fingers continued to pick at the seam of his coat while his lips moved in a soundless effort at expression.**

Notice that here the speaker whom you are quoting has failed, of his own volition, to complete the sentence. He was not interrupted. If he had been, you would have indicated that the break was a dramatic one (that is, involving opposition or conflict) by punctuating it with a pair of dashes.

> **"Well, I don't know about that," he replied. "There are so many problems, so many — " "But dammit, Grandfather," the young man broke in impatiently, "we have to be reasonable!"**

You will not have many occasions to use the three dots, but if you do use them, notice that they replace the words that are purposely omitted; therefore, they never absorb or are absorbed by another mark of punctuation.

> **"Blessed is the man," he read, "that walketh not in the council of the ungodly, nor standeth in the way of sinners, nor sitteth in the seat of the scornful. . . . He shall be like a tree planted by the rivers of water, that bringeth forth his fruit in his season. . . . The ungodly are not so, but are like the chaff which the wind driveth away."**

THE BAR (/)

The bar is so excessively rare that it might almost be omitted entirely from a book designed to help the average writer learn to punctuate effectively. Nevertheless, it is a mark of punctuation, it does have a meaning, and sometime in your life you may need it. Here it is, therefore, used in the only situation in which it ever occurs.

> **The student of poetic form has only to read such a passage as Bryant's "To him who in the love of nature holds/Communion with her visible forms, she speaks/A various language," to understand the use of run-on lines.**

The bar merely indicates the point at which a single verse of the poem is completed. It marks, in other words, the end of a rhythmic unit. Of course it is never used when poetry is printed as verse, for then the line ends are clearly shown by the disposition of the type. The bar is used only when poetry is printed straight along, like prose.

Do not confuse this punctuational use of the bar with its occasional use as a device of spelling.

Women and/or men may compete in the games.

This singularly clumsy Siamese twin of language, "and/or," is occasionally created, and when it is, it is spelled with the bar. You would do better to forget about it.

EXERCISE

1. When the wise man said vanity vanity ain't it the truth gushed Gussie all is vanity he must have been thinking about the new look an invention of the vicious demon if ever there was one what have women suffered for vanity yards of heavy stuff dustcatchers the bustle the no man can describe all the nonsense and all because there was no longer any money in the simple styles.

2. She was sentimental that morning and went around reciting when lovely woman stoops to folly and finds too late that men betray with meaningful glances in poor Edward's direction and he poor oaf began to feel guilty for what heaven only knows.

3. In his lecture on mixed metaphors the professor said when Shakespeare made Hamlet say to take arms against a sea of sorrows sic note the mixed metaphor and by opposing end them he was not thinking of the literary critic or college professor he was thinking of the paying customers.

4. If they do see thee they will murder thee is a line that is considered a test of an actress here Juliet must breathe forth terror and love and admiration no easy task in a single breathless line.

7
Some Non-Punctuational Symbols

THE ABBREVIATION POINT, THE HYPHEN, ETC.

You have already noted that some of the punctuation marks are occasionally used for non-punctuational purposes. For example, it was pointed out on page 6 that the *capital letter* is used in spelling proper names, and that it is also used frequently to indicate the beginning of a line of verse. On page 8, you noticed that a small dot, which looks exactly like a period, is used as an *abbreviation point* in the spelling of abbreviations. A similar small dot, this time called a *decimal point*, is used in spelling mixed numbers in Arabic figures (see p. 10). Also, there is the spelling symbol that looks exactly like a punctuational single comma (p. 19) and that is used in writing numerals larger than 999 in Arabic figures. And finally, there is the unique spelling use of the bar (p. 83).

In addition to these non-punctuational symbols that look like punctuation marks, there are certain other symbols frequently used in writing with which you should be familiar. One of them, the *hyphen*, has already been discussed (p. 63). It does not even look like any of the punctuation marks, for it is much shorter than the dash and quite unlike any of the others. Remember that it cannot be used for any punctuational purpose at all: it is purely and simply a device of spelling.

Besides the hyphen, there are two other non-punctuational symbols that should be noted: *underscoring* and the *apostrophe*. Again, they have nothing to do with punctuation, but it seems wise to discuss them briefly because so many people, including writers of textbooks, appear to believe that they do.

Underscoring

In hand-written or typed manuscripts, you frequently find words underscored. But had you noticed that you never see underscoring in printed matter? The reason is simple. When a writer draws a line under a word in his manuscript, he is simply making a little note to the printer: "Set this word up in italics." Never use this device unless, if your material were printed, you would want the underscored word to be italicized. The reason you underscore at all, of course, is that you cannot write or typewrite in italics.

What kinds of words should be italicized when printed, and therefore underlined in handwritten or typed manuscript? There are several groups of them, but the most important are these:

1. words in a foreign language;
2. titles of books, bound volumes, magazines, and newspapers;
3. words to which the writer wishes to call particular attention, either for emphasis or for some other purpose.

The Apostrophe (')

This small symbol, which looks like a single comma placed up above the line, is another device used in spelling. Its primary purpose is to indicate that in spelling a word you have omitted one or more letters. Therefore, one common situation in which the apostrophe occurs is in the spelling of contractions. For ex ample, the contracted form of "can not" is spelled "can't," and that of "it has" or "it is" is "it's."

The contraction of "will not" is "won't," and this brings up a curious question. Why is it not "win't?" The answer, like that to many other odd problems in English spelling, lies far back in the history of our language. In earlier periods, English-speaking people did not say "will not"; they said "woll not." This was logically contracted to "won't," and the old pronunciation and spelling of the contraction have held on right up to the present day, although the word "woll" has long since changed to "will."

A similar historical change in our language accounts for another common use of the apostrophe. We spell the possessive form of most nouns by adding an apostrophe and an *s* to the nominative (subject) form. Thus, if we want to express the idea that a hat belongs to a particular man, we write "the man's hat." Now the reason for this spelling is that the apostrophe indicates that we have omitted one or more letters, and here again we are merely writing a very old contraction. Centuries ago, English-speaking people used the form "mannes" to show possession, and they pronounced it as two syllables. Gradually they began to slur over the second syllable in speech and later wrote a contracted form that looked more like what they spoke. In this way, we got our form, "man's."

Normally, to spell the possessive form of a plural noun, we just add an apostrophe to the plural nominative ("the boys' hats"). But the whole question of spelling contractions and plurals in English is somewhat complicated, and cannot be adequately treated in a book about punctuation. When you have any doubt about the spelling of these or any other words, you should consult a good spelling book or dictionary.

8
Suggested Solutions to Exercises

The following suggestions are not offered as hard and fast "correct answers." They are indications of the way one person would solve the problems presented by the examples in the exercises. As you check through them, comparing them with your own solutions, remember that the purpose of punctuation is to make clear what the writer intended his sentence to mean. The meaning *you* would wish to communicate may be quite different, in which event you must either punctuate the same words differently or recast the sentence into your own words.

PAGE 20

1. We have fought with courage; our opponents, with guile.
2. It was a cold, clear day.
3. There was really nothing to do on the island except to swim, to hunt, or to fish.
4. He was very old, withered and brittle as an autumn leaf and as ready to be blown away.

   (If you insert an extra comma before the last "and," you will obscure the meaning: "withered," "brittle," and "as ready to be blown away" form a triple compound, all modified by "as an autumn leaf.")

5. It embraces such factors as food supplies, animal enemies, and even social traditions, customs, and laws.

6. The bodies of many animals are better adapted than man's for self-defense, escape, or hunting. Yet man has learned how to beat the polar bear, the hare, the hawk, and the tiger at their particular tricks.

7. The King of Norway, the Queen of England and Head of the Commonwealth, and the President of France were at the conference.

8. Wynken, Blynken, and Nod were sued for copyright infringement together, separately, and severally.

9. His sisters and his cousins and his aunts also went below.

10. The lame, the deaf, the dumb, and the blind came thronging to meet the new swami.

11. How many pesos equal one dollar? How many francs, one peso? How many lire, one franc?

12. Two weeks have been spent in planning; four, in getting the material together; sixteen, in consulting with various and sundry; and yet the work is not started.

(Some careful writers would omit the single commas here. They would argue that any reader would *understand* "weeks have been spent" at the two points where it is omitted, just as we frequently write sentences in which the subject is clearly understood and need not be stated.)

13. I've been so busy lately arranging for the hall, the printing of the tickets, the hiring of the musicians, the publicity in the newspapers and magazines and on the billboards that I've not been able to answer your kind, thoughtful letter.

(If you mean to stress only your "busy-ness" and intend the explanation of your activities to be purely parenthetical, put a pair of commas around the entire element that begins with "arranging" and ends with "billboards." See 22 on THE PAIR OF COMMAS.)

Page 29

1. Music, when soft voices die,
Vibrates in the memory.
Odors, when sweet violets sicken,
Live within the sense they quicken.

2. Peter, who was seven, and Nora, who was two, took turns on the sled.

3. Peter the Hermit was a far cry from Peter the Prior.

4. And so ends the story of Hansel and Gretel.

5. Henry, with his typical disregard or unawareness of the consequences, blustered on.

6. The Twentieth Air Force, which dropped the atom bomb, operated from the Marianas. The plane that carried the bomb was a special B-29.

7. He prayeth best who loveth best
All things both great and small.

(In the standard editions of "The Rime of the Ancient Mariner," either Coleridge or his editor has inserted a comma in the middle of the first line. It cannot be a single comma, and if it is intended as one part of a pair of commas it is plainly wrong. Even if it is the old-fashioned "musical notation" intended to suggest that the reader make a very slight pause, it is certainly uncalled for. I can see no sense in using any comma.)

8. "I want the following at the pool tomorrow: Joe, who admits he needs the practice; Fred, who won't admit it; and all those who think they are too good for the drudgery of training."

9. Can you remember the bell that used to ring whenever there was a fire?

10. After many a summer dies the swan.

or

After many a summer, dies the swan.

(There are two possible meanings, and the punctuation shows which you intend. Without the pair of commas, "After many a summer" is an essential modifier of "dies": you are making a point about the long life of the swan. If you use the pair of commas, you show the reader that your primary point is simply the swan's death, and that "After many a summer" is a nonessential element parenthetically added.)

11. Enemies and detractors, who do not know a hawk from a handsaw, will try to break your confidence in yourself.

(**Punctuated thus, the meaning is that all enemies and detractors are stupid. If you intended to say that only stupid enemies and detractors will try to break one's confidence, but that the clever ones will use some other method of defeating one, then the dependent clause would be essential to your meaning and would not have any commas around it.**)

12. The boy, upon hearing of the death of his adored elder brother, broke into a long, uncontrollable sob.

Page 31

1. The point, then, is to anticipate your partner's bid.
2. The job, you see, is to reload immediately.
3. He made up his mind, therefore, to hold his tongue and, come what might, to think things through alone.
4. "I'll go easy, if you know what I mean, if you'll reconsider buying the ticket."
5. The trouble, you'll agree, lies in ourselves, not in our stars.
6. And who, come to think of it, will be ready to carry on in your place?

Page 33

1. God bless you each and every one, large, small, and intermediate.
2. His generosity, or rather his recklessness, is a constant source of irritation to his wife.
3. Transcendentalism, the philosophy that has one foot in Platonism and the other in Christianity, depends on poetry for its full definition.
4. President Roosevelt said that the date of December 7, 1941, when the Japanese attacked Pear Harbor, would live in infamy.
5. The blow fell on the 30th of September in 1949.
6. R. H. Davis, reporter and soldier of fortune, seemed to enjoy the panoply of war.
7. Mr. Abernethy, the new minister for colonies, did not relinquish his old post of commissioner of the bureau of seed distribution.

8. And why should I listen to this, of all the demands, just and unjust, made upon my time?

   (Note that here you have a pair of commas within another pair.)

9. I cannot grant you, a student, a favor such as this one which I have refused Dr. Gammerton, my own colleague.

10. The company is one of the oldest Gary, Ind., enterprises.

Page 37

1. Your ancestry cannot help you, whatever it is.

2. If you feel, whatever your background, that you cannot stand and say, "Amen," then you must indeed search your heart.

   (Pairs within pairs. Notice that there is a pair of commas around the entire introductory clause: the first part of it has been absorbed by the capital letter and the second has merged with the final part of the pair of commas around "Amen.")

3. Of a' the airts the wind can blaw, I dearly like the west.

4. Of the thirteen who led the attack, the first two who died were the bravest.

   (Punctuated thus, this means that the bravest men were the two who died first, even though they may not have been the first to attack. If you mean that the bravest were the two who attacked first, then "who died" becomes purely parenthetical and nonessential and should be set off by a pair of commas.)

5. "To that question there is no answer," the old professor, wiping his glasses, replied.

6. The cook bellowed, "Come and get it!" in his belly-deep roar.

7. "All right, then, let it slide," said the weary officer of the day.

8. Although he advanced through calculation or shrewdness, his brother owed his promotion to outstanding courage, or recklessness, one might call it.

9. They were forced to act like beasts and not like men or women.

10. Although you prefer the thin sliced lamb, I like the beef, however you slice it.

11. Came the dawn, and there was Miss Mary Moppet, who was the child star of 1936.

12. The party of the first part hereby contracts to convey to the party of the second part and to his heirs and assigns, wherever they may be, all property, real or personal, on that site.

13. All he could say when he won the puppy was "Gosh!"

14. "No, you can't take it with you" was the platitude he ended with.

Page 43

1. It is true that she needs to sleep, but I still think we should wake her after six hours.

2. Day in and day out, the mailman made his rounds, and every day Henry's box was left empty.

3. Those who have read the assignment and those who have not will all be required to take the examination.

4. Either you will take the milk bottles to the store, or I shall have to go myself.

5. He walked far out onto the dock and stood there a long time staring at the water.

6. The old woman, who never in her life had been the center of so much attention, sat staring at the circle of kindly, anxious faces for a long moment, and then suddenly she burst into tears.

7. When the cat's away, the mice will play, for the natural instincts will be dominant.

8. Mr. Jackson, the newly elected deacon, read the first lesson, but the second lesson was delivered as usual by old Dr. Brown, who chanted in the same ringing tones we had heard for thirty years.

Page 50

1. He decided to leave early; therefore, he set the alarm, but of course he slept right through it.

(There are naturally other possible ways of punctuating these three clauses.)

2. Whenever the students play there are cheers and catcalls; when the old gentlemen play there is a dignified silence.

(Notice that in both clauses the subject is indefinite; it is for this reason that the introductory phrases, although out of place, are regarded as essential to the construction of a meaningful sentence and are not set off by pairs of commas. Some writers, however, do use the pair of commas in this kind of situation, probably without noticing whether the phrases are essential or nonessential.)

3. If the snow continues, the west will be isolated; without hope of new supplies by road transport, the town will have to rely on air drop.

4. We're with you, whatever happens; win, lose, or draw, you can do no wrong.

5. There was little to be done; they could thank their stars they were alive.

6. They failed to define their terms; therefore their argument aroused heat but no light.

7. We cannot hope to win, I admit, with so little preparation; nevertheless, we have no choice but to try.

Page 53

1. It is amazing how quickly we adapted ourselves to army life: to march and to groan and sing at once; to dig and to fill in what we dug; to get up with a bugle and, without time to dress, to fall out completely awake; to obey and to goldbrick with equal insouciance.

2. The airplane is a wonderful instrument of cooperating contradictions. Its speed is its safety; its height, its money in the bank; its turn is made with both rudder and stick, the more stick the less rudder; when you lose speed, you aim for the ground; and recover flaps must be used for takeoff, and mustn't be forgotten when you want to land or have to.

3. When I stop to consider, everything that grows seems to have its moment of mystery; every manifestation of nature conspires to fill us with awe; but we are soon

brought down to earth by its most trivial denizens. A flea, a mosquito, a gnat, which have not read the poets, will perform their workaday interruptions.

Page 58

1. I never heard the likes: babies squalling, radio blaring, pots clashing, and the older children shouting to make themselves heard. I hope never to hear such a racket again.

   (To avoid unpleasant rambling, make two sentences of this.)

2. The conductor announced a rather unimaginative program: Brahms, Tchaikowsky, and Franck.

3. The teacher's announcement of the marks aroused a groan: no A's, 3 B's, 4 C's, and the rest F's.

4. Miss Gray, take the following letter: "Dear Dr. Abernethy: Whenever you can, you are welcome to come visit our school, especially the gymnasium and the dining room; and the quadrangle and the theater are particularly attractive."

5. Whoever you are, this caution is directed toward you: a house cannot stand and live half free and half terrorized.

Page 62

1. Man or mouse—well, what are you? Make up your mind.

2. Money, clothes, and boy friends—is that all that's ever on your mind?

3. Friend or foe? Speak up, man.

4. There's no end to human misery. Birth shock, the terrors of childhood, the disappointments of youth—these we must all suffer, and try to fit ourselves into what we know we are if we would achieve a happy world.

5. And don't expect me to come to your rescue, whatever you've done, and I expect the worst: borrowing beyond your allowance, teasing the girls, and striking out with two men on. I must start letting nature take its course.

6. "The war to end wars"—who takes that phrase seriously any more?

7. Liberty or death—that was the choice Patrick Henry dramatically made. Because the occasion called for dramatic action, the young hillsman did not miss his opportunity.

Page 68

1. Wherever he is (and I'm not sure he's alive at all), he'll have to revisit the scene of his crime. Then we'll have our chance, after all these years, to nab the culprit. But whatever he's done (and he's done plenty), we shall try to forgive. But forget? Never.

2. Although this point has raised much controversy (*cf.* Miller, *op. cit.*, p. 39), there is no doubt that the author presents his material with masterly scholarship (*v.* p. 84).

3. I don't think you can really be so cruel as to recommend drowning them, if that's what I understood you to say.

4. At this time of year (and isn't it a lovely day?), you can expect to see at least a dozen kinds of birds all busy making nests (or stealing them, if the tradition about the cuckoo has any basis in fact).

    (In place of the first pair of parentheses in this sentence, many writers would prefer to use the pair of dashes. See p. 69 on THE PAIR OF DASHES.)

5. The only thing left is to attack before dawn. Or wouldn't you agree, Colonel?

6. The coach threw in all his reserves (all three of them).

7. If you or any of your accomplices are found skulking around here again, there will be the dickens to pay (plus a nice, fat fine).

Page 72

1. If you insist on acting this way—Gosh! I wish I had had the bringing up of you — there's no knowing where you'll end (in a ditch, most likely, dead drunk).

2. The hue and cry that arose, no matter how absurd and hysterical, was the result of a carefully planned heightening of tension.

3. Whenever I brought up the subject of a raise (and I was not as bashful then as I seem to be now), he started

telling me his baby's latest tricks or his latest off-color joke—anything to change the subject.

(Notice that this is the single dash, and not one of a pair.)

4. The New York celebrity, who is Manhattan-born — how you gonna keep 'em down on the farm?—is as rare as the champion baseball player who was born in the town he represents.

5. If we had world enough, and time — Oh, there's no use thinking about it. But the world is what it is, and who ever had time for one umpteenth of what he wanted to do (assuming that we ever really know what we want)?

Page 79

1. The ancient folk were wise, and had an old saw for every occasion; but we need wisdom, too, to choose between conflicting advice. "A stitch in time saves nine" is not quite the same as "Look before you leap."

2. Say it this way: "How now, brown cow?"

3. "You can't mean it," she panted. "I can't, can't I?" he replied with a melodramatic sneer. "Then take a look at this."

4. I read your last article, "Color Television is Here to Stay" in *Everyman's* magazine, and I wish I had your faith in science. But "wait and see" is my motto.

5. I heard you say, "There is little in Coleridge beyond 'Kubla Khan' and 'The Ancient Mariner' "; but I must ask you, "What about 'Christabel' and the volume called *Biographia Literaria?*"

6. "Where will all this soul-searching lead?" the lecturer asked. But did he ask, "Where shall a civilization go without soul-searching?"

Page 84

1. "When the wise man said, 'Vanity, vanity —' "
"Ain't it the truth?" gushed Gussie.
" '— all is vanity,' he must have been thinking about the 'new look,' an invention of the vicious demon, if ever there was one. What have women suffered for vanity? Yards of heavy stuff, dustcatchers, the bustle, the — no man can describe all the nonsense. And all because there was no longer any money in the simple styles."

2. She was sentimental that morning and went around reciting, "When lovely woman stoops to folly, / And finds too late that men betray," with meaningful glances in poor Edward's direction; and he, poor oaf, began to feel guilty — for what, heaven only knows.

3. In his lecture on mixed metaphors, the professor said, "When Shakespeare made Hamlet say, 'To take arms against a sea of sorrows [*sic!*]' — note the mixed metaphor — 'and by opposing end them,' he was not thinking of the literary critic or college professor; he was thinking of the paying customers."

4. "If they do see thee, they will murder thee" is a line that is considered a test of an actress. Here Juliet must breathe forth terror and love and admiration — no easy task in a single, breathless line.

9
Summary for Quick Reference

Punctuation: the art or practice of inserting standardized marks or signs in written matter to clarify the meaning and separate structural units.
— Webster's Collegiate Dictionary

Each of the standard marks is a conventional symbol with a definite meaning, just as a written word is a symbol with a definite meaning. Furthermore, each mark has one meaning and only one, and it is a meaning not communicated by the word-symbols alone. If you write "He died." your sentence means one thing; if you write "He died?" it has quite a different meaning. The only rule that will help you punctuate your writing effectively is simply this: understand what each mark means, just as you understand the meaning of each word-symbol you use, and then write what you intend to communicate.

BEGINNING AND END PUNCTUATION

The major structural unit in written English is the single sentence. If two or more sentences are run together without punctuation, the result is a meaningless jumble. To separate sentences as clearly defined units of thought, we use four familiar marks.

Capital Letter (A)   This familiar mark means that *at this point a new sentence begins.*

Note: Do not confuse this mark of punctuation with the non-punctuational capital letter used in *spelling* proper names nor with the capital letter often printed at the beginning of a line of verse. Since these do not affect meaning, they are not marks of punctuation.

Period (.)   *This is the end of a complete statement (declarative sentence).*

Note: Do not confuse with the *abbreviation point* (a device of *spelling* which shows that a particular group of letters is not a completed word-symbol but only a "shorthand" form of the word), nor with the *decimal point* (another *spelling* device used when we write a decimal fraction in Arabic figures).

Mr.   Okla.   Y.M.C.A. $2.57   0.008

Question Mark (?)   *This completed sentence asks a question.*

Where did you go on your holiday?

Exclamation Point (!)   *This completed sentence is expressed with great forcefulness.* If spoken, it should be exclaimed.

Keep away from the cliff!

Sentence Fragments   If you write a fragmentary or incomplete sentence (a word, phrase, or dependent clause) which makes complete sense by itself, treat it as a sentence and punctuate the beginning and end accordingly.

As you were.   Fire!   So what?

THE FIVE PRINCIPAL INTERIOR MARKS

The meaning of a sentence in English depends entirely on the order in which the words are arranged: *subject* with its essential modifiers, *verb* with its essential modifiers, *object or verb complement* with its essential modifiers. When the various elements are so arranged, the meaning is perfectly clear and no interior punctuation is needed. Occasionally the subject-predicate order can be completely reversed without confusing the reader. (*Example:* At the end of the road stood Dr. Miller's house.) But if it is changed in any other way, by omission, interjection, or compounding, the reader must be warned.

Single Comma (,)

At this point a small element is omitted, which can be easily supplied by the reader.

Reading maketh a full man; conference, a ready man; and writing, an exact man.

The element whose omission is most commonly indicated by the single comma is the conjuction joining words or phrases in a series.

The house was large, handsome, imposing.

or

The house was large, handsome, and imposing.

Though the final *and* is not omitted, the second single comma makes it clear that there are three elements in the series.

Pair of Commas (, . . . ,)

This is *one single mark of punctuation* composed of two symbols which are always separated from each other by a word or group of words. *The pair of commas encloses an element which, not being an essen-*

tial part of the sentence, interrupts or changes the normal order.

John, who never stopped to think before he acted, ran off immediately towards the firehouse.

Contrast with: One who never stops to think before he acts is apt to do some foolish things.

The girl, as you say, dances well.

This question, ladies and gentlemen, must be considered.

Thomas Jefferson was born in Albemarle County, Virginia, on April 13, 1743, according to our present calendar.

Johnny was shouting, "Last one in is a rotten egg," as he dived into the pool.

A direct quotation is generally regarded as a nonessential, interruptive element, though this usage seems purely conventional.

Note: When the nonessential, interruptive element is at the beginning or end of the sentence, only one part of the pair of commas is written; the other is absorbed by the stronger punctuation mark of capital letter or end mark.

As a matter of fact, this pie is not very good. I have eaten better pies, as a matter of fact.

Comma-Plus-Coordinating-Conjunction (, and)	This *single mark of punctuation* composed of two symbols is used *to join two independent clauses* (complete sentences) *into one compound sentence.*

The ladies wore their finest clothes, but the men wore business suits.

> **We must hurry, for time is of the essence.**

Semicolon (;) This mark has *exactly the same meaning and usage as the comma-plus-coordinating-conjunction;* either shows the midpoint of a compound sentence.

> **The ladies wore their finest clothes; the men wore business suits.**

<u>Note:</u> Sometimes, for complete clarity of meaning or for purely rhetorical effect, the single comma can be raised to a semicolon, and the comma-plus-conjunction can be changed to a semicolon-plus-conjunction. (See page 47.)

Colon (:) *The words following this mark will explain more fully the statement that precedes it.*

> **He asked me to bring three articles: a broom, a brush, and a rag.**

> **His manners were inexcusable: he screamed, leapt out of the chair, and thumbed his nose at the dentist.**

<u>Note:</u> It is conventional to place a colon after the salutation in a formal letter or speech.

> **Dear Sir: Madam President, Ladies and Gentlemen:**

RARELY NEEDED INTERIOR MARKS

Single Dash (—) The reverse of the colon, this mark means that *the preceding elements in this sentence explain more fully the statement now to be made.*

> **A broom, a brush, and a rag — these are the articles he asked me to bring.**

<u>Note:</u> Do not confuse the single dash with the much smaller *hyphen,* a spelling de-

vice used to join two or more words into one compound word, or at the end of a line when a word is broken into syllables.

a three-year-old child   **forty-seven**

Parentheses
(. . .)
A stronger, more noticeable mark than the pair of commas, *parentheses enclose a nonessential, interruptive element which has little, if any, grammatical relation to the rest of the sentence.*

The capital city (population 750,000) was placed under martial law.

Pair of
Dashes
(— . . . —)
This very emphatic mark encloses a nonessential element which interrupts the normal order of the sentence with great violence, either syntactical or emotional.

Under the growing pressure of population — London's increased from around 100,000 at the beginning of Elizabeth's reign to double that number under her successor — the city had spread beyond the old walls.

As with the pair of commas, but never with the parentheses, sometimes only the first half of the pair of dashes is written. This is true when a partial sentence is violently broken off and never completed.

"Look out!" she screamed. "We are — " The roar of the motor drowned her voice.

Note: The pair of dashes has recently become the most grossly misused and over-used of all the marks of punctuation, usually in place of the much milder parentheses or the still less disturbing pair of commas. Note carefully the degree of interruption indicated by each of these three marks, and use the pair of dashes sparingly.

PUNCTUATION OF QUOTED MATTER

Quotation Marks
("...")
('...')

The element enclosed in quotation marks comprises the exact words of someone whom the author is quoting. The single quotation marks enclose a quotation within a quotation.

"Julius Caesar," said Professor Smith, "was always ready to boast, 'I came, I saw, I conquered,' whenever he had burned some miserable village and massacred its inhabitants."

Brackets
[...]

The element enclosed within a pair of brackets is an explanatory remark inserted into the quotation by the quoter.

According to the stenographic record, the Representative became very angry. "If the gentleman would spend some time in my part of the country," he shouted, "he would find that people of Niles and Hampton [small towns in the speaker's district] look with contempt upon his proposals!"

Three Dots
(...)

At this point, certain elements are omitted from the quotation, but without any suggestion of violence.

The question that bothered Hamlet was, as he said, "Whether 'tis nobler in the mind to suffer ... or to take arms."

"Well, it is hard, but I ..." His voice trailed away into an inaudible whisper.

The Bar (/)

Although the quotation is printed as prose, this mark *indicates the end of a single line of verse.*

A passage such as Bryant's "To him who in the love of nature holds / Communion with her visible forms, she speaks / A various language" illustrates the use of run-on lines.

SOME NON-PUNCTUATIONAL DEVICES

There are several small symbols used in writing and printing which, although most of them look exactly like one or another of the punctuation marks, have nothing to do with punctuation, since they do not in any way clarify the meaning and structure of sentences.

Capital Letter Used in spelling proper names and to indicate the beginning of a line of verse.

Abbreviation Point. The small dot used in spelling abbreviations.

Decimal Point. The small dot used in spelling mixed numbers.

Comma in Numbers. A comma-like symbol used in writing large numbers in Arabic figures.

Hyphen. A small symbol used to join two or more words into one compound word, or at the end of a line when a word is broken into syllables.

Apostrophe. A symbol which looks like a comma written or printed above the line; used only within a word-symbol, it indicates the omission of one or more letters, contractions, and possessives.

Underscoring. Used in preparing a manuscript for printing, it indicates that the underlined word or words should be set in italics.

10
Exercises
for Practice

"Practice makes perfect" may be a trite and well-worn saying, but it is nevertheless true. The following exercises are designed to enable you to use your knowledge of the system of punctuation explained in this book. First, study the list below of the various situations in which punctuation is used. Then study a set of correctly punctuated sentences and choose from the list the appropriate reason for the correct punctuation. This exercise should not be difficult, but it will serve to reinforce the system in your mind. Later you will progress to an exercise that asks you to supply the correct marks of punctuation.

The punctuation indicates

A. omission of small elements, such as coordinating conjunctions, from a sentence

B. omission of a small element from a *series* of words or phrases in the same construction

C. an element, such as a transitional word or phrase, not grammatically essential to the construction of the sentence

D. elements in apposition

E. the enclosing of a direct quotation

F. the enclosing of nonessential elements at the beginning or end of a sentence

G. a coordinating conjunction joining two independent clauses

H. the joining of two independent clauses *without* a coordinating conjunction

I. a series of long and complicated elements, in at least some of which there is interior punctuation

J. that the words which immediately follow the mark of punctuation will give a fuller explanation of what has just been stated

K. that the preceding elements in the sentence explain more fully the statement made after the mark of punctuation

L. that the enclosed element interrupts the formal flow of thought violently

M. the separation of items in a series using "and"

EXERCISE 1:

Place the appropriate letter from the above list, indicating the type of punctuation used, in the blank at the left of the following correct sentences. In cases where more than one type of punctuation is used, place each appropriate letter in the blank.

_____ **1.** The committee asked that Thomas Stinton, Director of Parks and Recreation, be summoned for questions.

_____ **2.** The birds were chirping merrily, and the dew on the grass was sparkling in the morning light.

_____ **3.** I have four favorite Broadway shows: *My Fair Lady, Oklahoma, West Side Story,* and *The King and I.*

_____ **4.** The composer's last work, a concerto for tuba, was not well received by the critics.

_____ **5.** He began to cry out, not as though in pain but in anguish.

_____ **6.** The woman by the checkout counter, it seems, may be concealing stolen merchandise.

_____ 7. Joan complained, "I didn't think Egypt would be so terribly hot at this time of the year."

_____ 8. No one said a word, and some of the class seemed to be holding their breath.

_____ 9. Horace was very upset; Julia seems much more capable of coping with her anger.

_____ 10. Magic Johnson is the greatest basketball player—never mind about Larry Bird—in the whole wide world.

_____ 11. The agenda called for an interview with John Barton, the head of external operations; a discussion of city taxes; and a report from the marketing division.

_____ 12. No one at the office had ever heard of Thomas Hardy, and they laughed when I told them my favorite novel is *The Return of the Native*.

_____ 13. We cannot say why we do not want to do this thing; we just feel very strongly that we should not.

_____ 14. Mrs. Hopkins was in a dilemma: she could neither move forward nor step backward.

_____ 15. The vaccination, therefore, is necessary if we want to avoid an epidemic and many deaths.

_____ 16. The thin, weak, emaciated man was the sensation of the weight-loss class.

_____ 17. Let us hear from Gladys Forbish, the lead soprano, in the next number.

_____ 18. As I understand it, no one who has previously been suspended will be allowed to compete in the upcoming tournament.

_____ 19. Caitlin yelled, "Don't tell me how to fry eggs," and dumped out the contents of the frying pan.

_____ 20. A good plot, interesting characters, and sparkling dialogue—all these make up an interesting novel.

_____ **21.** There is nothing so delicious as ice cream, and there is nothing more fattening.

_____ **22.** Sarah loved to sing, not with words but with a kind of humming.

_____ **23.** In my opinion, one who cannot keep a straight face while reading poetry should not be called upon to recite.

_____ **24.** Judy had three things she feared most: thunder, lightning, and windstorms.

_____ **25.** Paul Adams, the janitor, will assist in setting up the exhibit.

_____ **26.** The principal task, however, will be the planning of the event.

_____ **27.** Never wait until the last minute; always write your papers ahead of time.

_____ **28.** It seemed like the longest day of her life to Alice: everything that could go wrong occurred.

_____ **29.** We cannot survive as a nation without doctors, who supply medical care; lawyers, who regulate our actions through the courts; and educators, who give the doctors and lawyers the knowledge required to do their jobs.

_____ **30.** Hot sun, white beach sand, and ocean waves— this is my idea of a spring vacation.

_____ **31.** The hot, dusty, impoverished village was typical of the ones that explorers found in the interior.

_____ **32.** No one should think, however, that the students in the lower grades are unimportant.

_____ **33.** The town had its problems, but there were none that were impossible to solve.

_____ **34.** Call Jacobs, the plumber, and tell him it is an emergency.

_____ **35.** Do not complain about your lack of luxuries; there are those who have nothing.

_____ **36.** Joan was a brunette; Joyce, a blonde.

_____ **37.** "Yes," said Brandon politely.

_____ **38.** Believe me, this kind of foolishness is going to have to come to a grinding halt.

_____ **39.** Bright lights, the sound of traffic, and the energy of the people moving in the streets—this is city life to me.

_____ **40.** The full, rich, harmonious chords of the symphony orchestra delighted her.

_____ **41.** What are you doing—hey, wait a minute—with that firecracker?

_____ **42.** "Thirty days has September," Julius replied.

_____ **43.** I do not wish to participate, but I would like to watch.

_____ **44.** For once, I want to see a really exciting movie about chess.

_____ **45.** Find the job that you really enjoy doing; you will then find that success comes easily.

_____ **46.** Finding the right job, however, is not always easy.

_____ **47.** When will Mr. Smith, our principal, learn to appreciate rock music?

_____ **48.** We are not amused by this action: throwing food cannot be tolerated in a civilized society.

_____ **49.** Polly wanted a cracker; Rover, a bone.

_____ **50.** We must not neglect George, who has a reading problem; Harry, who is weak in math; or Betty, who cannot pass the physical education requirement.

EXERCISE 2:

Add the correct punctuation marks to the following sentences. Also complete the blank at the left of each sentence by filling in the appropriate letter (or letters) from the list of rules on pages 108–109, designating the type of punctuation used.

_____ 1. The proper solution to most problems however is based on logic and common sense.

_____ 2. Never step on people on the way up you will meet these same people on the way down.

_____ 3. Those present were Joanne Hayes Director of Freshman English Lena Hensley Director of Public Relations and John Moses a professor.

_____ 4. Jim preferred a comedy Jane a serious movie.

_____ 5. Jackson High School had a good record in all sports but Jefferson High excelled only in basketball.

_____ 6. The proper sauces the correct spices and the precise time of cooking all these are necessary for gourmet dishes.

_____ 7. The cold icy windswept weather made it uncomfortable to sit and watch the football game.

_____ 8. Finally be aware of the possibility of failure.

_____ 9. Ken knew only one thing to do confess his error immediately.

_____ 10. He was acting crazy if you know what I mean and jumping up and down and waving his arms and hooraying as though we'd just won the state championship.

_____ 11. Norman Mailer the novelist and fighter will read from his works at the auditorium tonight.

_____ 12. I have no interest in professional sports and I never watch them on television.

_____ 13. The long tiresome tedious hours on the job made Henry weary.

_____ 14. John asked Why do you want to go to Tahiti?

_____ 15. The wounded soldier had only one thing in mind crawling to safety behind the American lines.

_____ 16. It can never be the same too much has happened to change it.

_____ 17. For us this is a great dinner.

_____ **18.** If you wish to argue a favorite pastime of yours then go somewhere else.

_____ **19.** Beth could not eat foods with cholesterol and Bob could eat no sweets.

_____ **20.** When is the last time you saw Sean the tall boy with the long hair or Jim the one who played drums at the last party or Larry the one who acted so silly?

_____ **21.** The small boy was excited the little girl calm.

_____ **22.** Plenty of vegetables and fruit fresh air and exercise this is my road to good health.

_____ **23.** Is this the story about Tess the poor girl who died tragically?

_____ **24.** Cold uncooked tasteless frankfurters is not my favorite dish.

_____ **25.** The answer therefore is right in front of your nose.

EXERCISE 3:

Add the correct punctuation to the sentences in the following paragraph.

[1]There was a small sliver of a moon visible in the eastern sky and the wind had diminished to a slight breeze.

[2]Listen Curt said do you hear the low soft mournful sound coming from the woods?

[3]I listened for several minutes it stopped and then started again. [4]The sound could only come from one bird the mourning dove. [5]I wanted to stay and listen Curt to go. [6]In the group of hikers was Curt an old friend Pete a new acquaintance and me. [7]Getting away from the city breathing unpolluted air and hearing the sounds of nature these had brought us out on a balmy night. [8]Curt the biology professor at a local high school was our leader.

⁹Curt was persistent maybe this is too mild a word in urging us to get away from the city and enjoy the country. ¹⁰It is not that he was unpleasant he always made his requests in a humorous way. ¹¹Actually it was the sort of thing I looked forward to every spring. ¹²On this particular night however I found myself puffing a bit harder as I mounted the hills.

¹³I must be out of shape I said.

¹⁴Curt yelled back in that drill-sergeant tone of his that I have come to expect for me to shape up or ship out. ¹⁵Pete was puzzled Curt quietly laughing. ¹⁶He told me that a good hiker must have stamina stamina and more stamina. ¹⁷I told him that what I needed was rest and I sat down on the stump of an oak tree. ¹⁸Pete had brought along a thermos jug of hot steaming strong-smelling coffee.

¹⁹Now I know why we asked you to come along I said to him.

²⁰The coffee was terrible and provided only one thing warmth. ²¹The air was getting chilly now and we began to discuss the possibility of turning back. ²²It was then that we heard the strangest most frightening sound I had ever heard. ²³It sounded like a woman's cry of pain and terror I do not think I shall ever forget the sound. ²⁴Violence evil and tragedy these were the themes of the next hour of our lives. ²⁵I hope that everyone friend and foe alike will be spared this type of experience.

SOLUTIONS

EXERCISE 1

1. D	**11.** I	**21.** G	**31.** B	**41.** L
2. G	**12.** G	**22.** A	**32.** C	**42.** E
3. J, M	**13.** H	**23.** F	**33.** G	**43.** G
4. C	**14.** J	**24.** J, M	**34.** D	**44.** F
5. A*	**15.** C	**25.** D	**35.** H	**45.** H
6. C	**16.** B	**26.** C	**36.** A	**46.** C
7. E	**17.** D	**27.** H	**37.** E	**47.** D
8. G	**18.** F	**28.** J	**38.** F	**48.** J
9. H	**19.** E	**29.** I	**39.** K, M	**49.** A
10. L	**20.** K, M	**30.** K, M	**40.** B	**50.** I

* The comma in this sentence does indicate that a small element has been omitted; however, this practice, the A rule, differs from B in that there is no *series* of elements.

EXERCISE 2

C   **1.** The proper solution to most problems, however, is based on logic and common sense.

H   **2.** Never step on people on the way up; you will meet these same people on the way down.

I   **3.** Those present were Joanne Hayes, Director of Freshman English; Lena Hensley, Director of Public Relations; and John Moses, a professor.

A   **4.** Jim preferred a comedy; Jane, a serious movie.

G   **5.** Jackson High School had a good record in all sports, but Jefferson High excelled only in basketball.

K, M   **6.** The proper sauces, the correct spices, and the precise time of cooking—all these are necessary for gourmet dishes.

B   **7.** The cold, icy, windswept weather made it uncomfortable to sit and watch the football game.

F   **8.** Finally, be aware of the possibility of failure.

J 9. Ken knew only one thing to do: confess his error immediately.

L 10. He was acting crazy—if you know what I mean—and jumping up and down, and waving his arms, and hooraying as though we'd just won the state championship.

D 11. Norman Mailer, the novelist and fighter, will read from his works at the auditorium tonight.

G 12. I have no interest in professional sports, and I never watch them on television.

B 13. The long, tiresome, tedious hours on the job made Henry weary.

E 14. John asked, "Why do you want to go to Tahiti?"

J 15. The wounded soldier had only one thing in mind: crawling to safety behind the American lines.

H 16. It can never be the same; too much has happened to change it.

F 17. For us, this is a great dinner.

L 18. If you wish to argue—a favorite pastime of yours—then go somewhere else.

G 19. Beth could not eat foods with cholesterol, and Bob could eat no sweets.

I 20. When is the last time you saw Sean, the tall boy with the long hair; or Jim, the one who played drums at the last party; or Larry, the one who acted so silly?

A 21. The small boy was excited; the little girl, calm.

K, M 22. Plenty of vegetables and fruit, fresh air, and exercise—this is my road to good health.

D 23. Is this the story about Tess, the poor girl who died tragically?

B 24. Cold, uncooked, tasteless frankfurters is not my favorite dish.

C 25. The answer, therefore, is right in front of your nose.

EXERCISE 3

[1]There was a small sliver of a moon visible in the eastern sky, and the wind had diminished to a slight breeze.

[2]"Listen," Curt said, "do you hear the low, soft, mournful sound coming from the woods?"

[3]I listened for several minutes; it stopped and then started again. [4]The sound could only come from one bird: the mourning dove. [5]I wanted to stay and listen; Curt, to go. [6]In the group of hikers was Curt, an old friend; Pete, a new acquaintance; and me. [7]Getting away from the city, breathing unpolluted air, and hearing the sounds of nature—these had brought us out on a balmy night. [8]Curt, the biology professor at a local high school, was our leader. [9]Curt was persistent—maybe this is too mild a word—in urging us to get away from the city and enjoy the country. [10]It is not that he was unpleasant; he always made his requests in a humorous way. [11]Actually, it was the sort of thing I looked forward to every spring. [12]On this particular night, however, I found myself puffing a bit harder as I mounted the hills.

[13]"I must be out of shape," I said.

[14]Curt yelled back—in that drill-sergeant tone of his that I have come to expect—for me to shape up or ship out. [15]Pete was puzzled; Curt, quietly laughing. [16]He told me that a good hiker must have stamina, stamina, and more stamina. [17]I told him that what I needed was rest, and I sat down on the stump of an oak tree. [18]Pete had brought along a thermos jug of hot, steaming, strong-smelling coffee.

[19]"Now I know why we asked you to come along," I said to him.

[20]The coffee was terrible and provided only one thing: warmth. [21]The air was getting chilly now, and we began to discuss the possibility of turning back. [22]It was then that we heard the strangest, most frightening sound

I had ever heard. [23]It sounded like a woman's cry of pain and terror; I do not think I shall ever forget the sound. [24]Violence, evil, and tragedy—these were the themes of the next hour of our lives. [25]I hope that everyone, friend and foe alike, will be spared this type of experience.

The sentences above are punctuated according to the following rules (as found in the rule list on pages 108–109).

1. G	**9.** L	**17.** G
2. B, E	**10.** H	**18.** B
3. H	**11.** F	**19.** E
4. J	**12.** C	**20.** J
5. A	**13.** E	**21.** G
6. I	**14.** L	**22.** B
7. K, M	**15.** A	**23.** H
8. D	**16.** B	**24.** K, M
		25. C or D

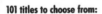

Notes

Notes